DAYS OF SORROW, YEARS OF GLORY

THE FUGITIVE'S SONG,

LITH. OF E.W. BOUVÉ BOSTON

WORDS
composed and respectfully dedicated, in token of confident esteem to

FREDERICK DOUGLASS
A Graduate from the
"PECULIAR INSTITUTION"

For his fearless advocacy, signal ability and wonderful success in behalf of
HIS BROTHERS IN BONDS.

(and to the **FUGITIVES FROM SLAVERY** in the)
FREE STATES & CANADAS.
by their friend
JESSE HUTCHINSON JUNR.

BOSTON, Published by HENRY PRENTISS 33 Court St.

Entered according to act of congress in the year 1845 by Henry Prentiss in the clerks office of the district court of Massachusetts.

MILESTONES IN BLACK AMERICAN HISTORY

DAYS OF SORROW, YEARS OF GLORY

1831–1850

FROM THE NAT TURNER REVOLT TO THE FUGITIVE SLAVE LAW

Timothy J. Paulson

CHELSEA HOUSE PUBLISHERS
New York   Philadelphia

SSCCA

FRONTISPIECE   Images of runaway slaves appeared in many forms during the mid-19th century. This one, which shows the celebrated antislavery activist and former slave Frederick Douglass, decorated the sheet music for "The Fugitive's Song," a popular ballad of 1845.

ON THE COVER   Led by their pastor, enslaved plantation workers take part in an emotional religious service. Even in captivity, African Americans maintained their spiritual freedom.

Chelsea House Publishers
Editorial Director   Richard Rennert
Executive Managing Editor   Karyn Gullen Browne
Copy Chief   Robin James
Picture Editor   Adrian G. Allen
Art Director   Robert Mitchell
Manufacturing Director   Gerald Levine

Milestones in Black American History
Senior Editor   Marian W. Taylor
Series Originator and Adviser   Benjamin I. Cohen
Series Consultants   Clayborne Carson, Darlene Clark Hine
Series Designer   Rae Grant

Staff for DAYS OF SORROW, YEARS OF GLORY
Editorial Assistant   Annie McDonnell
Picture Researcher   Pat Burns

3 5 7 9 8 6 4 2

Library of Congress Cataloging-in-Publication Data

Paulson, Timothy J.
    Days of sorrow, years of glory, 1831–1850 : from the Nat Turner revolt to the fugitive slave law / Timothy J. Paulson.
        p. cm. — (Milestones in Black American history)
    Includes bibliographical references and index.
        ISBN 0-7910-2263-3.
        ISBN 0-7910-2552-7 (pbk.)
    1. Slavery—United States—History—19th century. 2. Afro-Americans—History—To 1863. 3. United States—History—1815–1861. I. Title. II. Series.
E449.P333 1994
973'.0496073—dc20

93-40851
CIP

CONTENTS

MILESTONES IN BLACK AMERICAN HISTORY

INTRODUCTION

✳

America's Civil War began in 1861, but its first shots exploded 30 years earlier, when an enslaved black Virginian rose up and struck a thunderous blow for freedom. Nat Turner's astonishing 1831 revolt cost some 200 lives, engulfed southeast Virginia in flames, and spread stark terror across the slaveholding South. It also changed the course of American history.

Turner died at the end of a rope and Virginia's burning farms cooled, but the explosive power of the revolt did not. Reports of the daring action brought new hope and courage to blacks throughout the South: slaves who had hardly dared to dream of freedom now raised their eyes to the stars and started walking north. At the same time, frightened slaveholders sharply tightened their controls over the black population, worsening the very conditions that had helped fuel the revolt. The South's mounting racial harshness served to stiffen the resolve of the abolitionists, those northerners who were determined to end slavery at any cost. After Turner's revolt, America found itself on a collision course with war.

Crowding the next two decades were countless acts of bravery and betrayal, of savage repression and stoic resistance, of tyranny and generosity. And there were heroes—unnumbered and often unnamed—who, against overwhelming odds, fought for and won freedom for themselves and others. These were the years of the African American alliance with the Seminole Indians in a conflict with the United States—a "savage and negro war," according to President Andrew Jackson—that presented uncontestable proof of black valor and military skill. These were the years, too, of the Underground Railroad and its legendary "conductor," Harriet Tubman; of the Philadelphia Vigilance Committee's William Still, one courageous black man who saved thousands of others from slavery; and of the appearance of new and brilliant black leaders, many of them former slaves such as Frederick Douglass and Sojourner Truth, who worked to end slavery and put the black population in control of its own destiny. And in these years, black Americans carved niches in technology and the arts as well as in politics and antislavery actions.

This tumultuous period closed with the enactment of the Fugitive Slave Law of 1850, one of the most bitterly resented statutes ever passed in the United States. Designed as a compromise to keep the nation from flying apart, the act wound up endangering every black in America and pushing the nation even further toward civil conflict. Beginning with Turner's incredible bid for freedom and ending with the infamous law for fugitive slaves, the years from 1831 to 1850 set the young American republic on a new, more violent, but eventually higher road. It was an era that encompassed some of black American history's most dramatic and inspiring events.

MILESTONES
1831-50

1831

August: Revolution in Virginia

- Nat Turner of Southampton County, Virginia, leads eight fellow slaves in the most momentous rebellion ever staged in the United States. Costing the lives of some 60 whites and more than 140 blacks, the revolt creates panic in the slaveholding South and galvanizes both proslavery and abolitionist sentiment across the nation. Turner is captured in October and hanged on November 11.

June: Racist Violence in the North

- Liberal white schoolmistress Prudence Crandall opens an academy for "young colored Ladies and Misses" in Canterbury, Connecticut. Outraged neighbors harass teacher and pupils, break the school's windows, poison its well, and finally burn it to the ground.

December: Abolitionist Society Organized

- Meeting in Philadelphia, Pennsylvania, black and white abolitionists create a powerful new organization: the American Anti-Slavery Society.

1836

May: Congress Passes "Gag Rule"

- Giving in to southerners and conservative northerners, Congress passes a law tabling all discussion of slavery, thereby silencing opponents of slavery and depriving Americans of their traditional right to petition. (The law was repealed eight years later.)

1837

November: Martyrdom for an Abolitionist

- While trying to defend his printing press in Alton, Illinois, white abolitionist editor Elijah P. Lovejoy is murdered by a proslavery mob.

1838

An American in London

- Frank Johnson, one of America's first black bandmasters, takes his musicians to London's Buckingham Palace. Victoria, monarch of the British Empire, is reportedly "thrilled" by the American "Colored Band."

January: African-Indian Forces Defeated in Florida

- The long-running Seminole Wars grind to a halt when U.S. forces overcome a black-Indian army at the Battle of Lockahatchee. Before bowing to superior numbers and arms, the interracial military alliance had managed to keep the United States and its soldiers at bay for more than two decades in what President Andrew Jackson called "this savage and negro war." By 1843, the government had exiled the remnants of Florida's Seminole Indians and their black allies to the West.

August: First Black Magazine Appears

- Black abolitionist David Ruggles publishes the premiere copy of *Mirror of Liberty*, the nation's first magazine edited by and directed toward blacks, in New York City.

September: A Leader Emerges

- Future abolitionist speaker and writer Frederick Douglass escapes from slavery in Baltimore, Maryland.

1839

July: Slave Mutiny

- Joseph Cinque, a captured African en route to Cuba, leads his fellow prisoners in a spectacular revolt against the officers of the Spanish slave ship *Amistad*. The rebels are imprisoned by U.S. officials in Long Island, New York, but later are freed and allowed to return to their native land.

1841

American "Hot Music" Draws International Audience

- British novelist Charles Dickens is one of many celebrities who flock to New York City's "Five Points" to see the area's famous black musicians and entertainers. Among the most popular of these is William Henry Lane, billed as "Master Juba, the Greatest of all Dancers."

1842

November: Sailing to Freedom

- The slave ship *Creole*, en route from Hampton, Virginia, to New Orleans, Louisiana, is commandeered by her prisoners. After overcoming the ship's crew, the black rebels sail the vessel to the British-held Bahamas, where they are granted asylum and then freedom.

Abolitionist Sentiment in Ohio

- The U.S. Congress sharply rebukes Representative Joshua Giddings for praising the *Creole* rebels. Giddings resigns and returns to Ohio, where he is reelected by a landslide.

1843 June: A Mighty Voice Begins to Speak

- Sojourner Truth, a freed slave from New York State, begins her extraordinary career as an abolition crusader.

1846 Black Inventor Revolutionizes Industry

- Norbert Rillieux, a freeborn Louisianian, patents a new evaporation process that makes sugar whiter and grainier. Rillieux's invention will be widely adopted in sugar production as well as in many other industries.

1847 December: The *North Star* Lights Up

- Frederick Douglass publishes the first issue of his controversial and highly effective antislavery newspaper, the *North Star*, in Rochester, New York.

1849 Summer: "Moses" Leaves the Wilderness

- Harriet Tubman, the heroic Underground Railroad "conductor" who will lead more than 300 slaves to freedom and become known as the Moses of her people, makes her own escape from slavery in Maryland.

1850 September: Congress Explodes a Bombshell

- Congress enacts the Compromise of 1850, a sweeping new approach to the slavery "problem." Among the compromise's provisions is one that outlaws the slave trade in Washington, D.C.—but allows the city to retain slavery—and the passage of the new Fugitive Slave Law. Under this legislation, almost any white person claiming to be the owner of almost any black person can obtain a court order sending the black into slavery. Perhaps more than any other event or issue, the Fugitive Slave Law of 1850 galvanizes pro- and antislavery forces and pushes the nation closer to the civil war that will engulf it in 1860.

1

TWO DECADES OF STRUGGLE

SUNDAY, August 21, 1831, had been a scorcher in Southampton County, Virginia. And darkness brought no relief; at 2:00 A.M. sullen, sticky air still blanketed the countryside. Outside Joseph Travis's farmhouse, light from a flickering torch revealed seven silent men, grim, sweat-streaked, and black. They carried knives and axes.

The men knew the Travis family would be asleep after a day of neighborhood visiting; the time was ripe. Dousing the torch, they moved swiftly toward the clapboard farmhouse. On their way they were met and joined by two of the family's slaves. Pausing at the farm's cider press, the men bolstered their courage with a jolt of strong apple brandy. Then their leader, Nat Turner—the man they called the Prophet—began to speak softly. He asked them to make good their "valiant boastings, so often repeated." The group crossed the yard to the house.

Nat Turner—seen here in a portrait based on eyewitness descriptions—led America's most devastating slave revolt. His 1831 rebellion in Virginia spread stark terror throughout the slaveholding South.

13

A contemporary woodcut shows Turner (fourth from right) and his men in action. Agreeing to spare no whites— children, women, or men— the rebels left a trail of blood across southeastern Virginia.

Hark, Turner's broad-shouldered second-in-command, immediately began to chop at the door with his ax. Afraid the noise would give them away, Turner restrained him, climbed a ladder, and vanished into a second-story window. Moments later he appeared at the front door. "The work is now open to you," he whispered. The band slipped noiselessly into the house. Turner led the way, closely followed by Will, a slave from a nearby farm, into the master bedroom. There Turner's owner, Joseph Travis, lay asleep with his wife, Sally.

Because Turner was their leader, the men wanted him to strike the first blow. All seven were slaves, and with this act, they hoped, they would make their first step on the road to freedom. Turner raised his hatchet and struck out wildly in the shadowy darkness. The blade glanced off Travis's head; he woke up screaming and calling out his wife's name. Will swung his ax and cut the white man down, then hacked Sally Travis to pieces. After more than two centuries of bondage and oppression, the bloodiest rebellion in the history of southern slavery had begun.

The fighting and killing would rage for two more days. Under the steady leadership of Nat Turner, the rebel band would swell to nearly 80 people, and in the end more than 60 whites and some 140 blacks would die. Over the years that followed, this rebellion was to grow in significance and shape events that would change the course of American history.

The Turner revolt had its roots in more than two centuries of American life. Slavery had been practiced in America since the early 1600s, when European colonists realized they would need a vast pool of

Prospective buyers examine "merchandise" at a slave auction. Among the customers is one of the prewar South's strangest phenomena: a black slaveholder (sixth from the left). "Some free Negroes," notes black historian John Hope Franklin, "had a real economic interest in . . . slavery and held slaves in order to improve their own economic status."

laborers to work their large farms, or plantations. Soon slave traders were visiting the western coast of Africa, where they bought captured Africans, carried them across the Atlantic to America, and sold them at a profit. Through the labor of these enslaved Africans, the plantations swelled in size, requiring still more slaves to raise and harvest the crops. By the time of Turner's revolt, America's slave population numbered nearly 3 million.

Not all blacks in North America were slaves. By the 1830s many free blacks lived in the North, where people viewed slavery in a different light than did their southern cousins. Because its economy was urban and industrial rather than rural and agricultural, the North had little use for slave labor; factories needed fewer but more highly skilled workers than plantations required. The North, therefore, felt less threatened by the idea of abolishing "the peculiar institution," as many southerners called slavery. (The term was a short version of an older phrase, "the peculiar domestic institution of the South," whose origins are obscure. Such vague words helped cover up the embarrassment that even some slave owners felt at the mention of slavery.)

Often freeing their slaves voluntarily, many northern whites became abolitionists, people who believed that the practice of slavery should be ended. By 1808 the United States had outlawed the importation of slaves, but that did not halt the buying and selling of human beings within the country's boundaries. By the time of Turner's revolt, slavery was more vital to the southern economy than ever; in 1820 the South's cotton production provided more than half the value of all U.S. exports combined—and it was slaves who planted, processed, and harvested the cotton.

The South reeled under the impact of Nat Turner's revolt, which would push the nation toward the great civil war that engulfed it between 1860 and

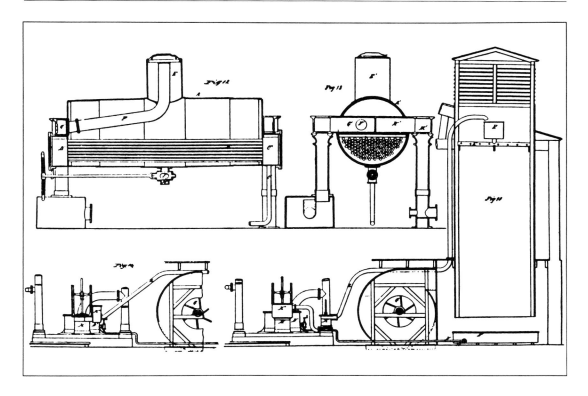

1865. And in the years between the revolt and passage of the Fugitive Slave Law of 1850, other events would push it still further. Those two decades of struggle produced a number of remarkable black achievers, men and women whose triumphs seem especially impressive because of the era that gave them birth and because they involved not only antislavery activism but the arts and sciences.

Norbert Rillieux, a black Louisiana inventor, patented this evaporating pan in 1846. Part of his new sugar-refining system, the device revolutionized the sugar industry and was later adapted for use in a number of other fields.

Among these achievers was Norbert Rillieux (1806–94), a freeborn native of New Orleans, Louisiana. Rillieux, who even as a boy showed an unusual talent for engineering, invented a technique known as the multiple-effect vacuum evaporation process, which would revolutionize the refining of sugar. First tested on a Louisiana

plantation in 1834, Rillieux's process failed, as it would again in 1841. But in 1845 the inventor improved his system, and sugar planters across the South began to install it. In about 1861 Rillieux moved to France, where in 1881 he perfected and unveiled the standard refining system still in worldwide use, not only in sugar production but in the manufacture of such products as condensed milk, glue, and gelatin.

By 1830 slavery had virtually disappeared in the North, but blacks still found themselves fettered by vast economic, educational, and social inequality. Some nevertheless began to compete in the arts and other fields previously closed to them. In the 1830s Newport Gardner, for example, became well known in New England, where he operated what one observer called a "very numerously attended singing school," an institution that enrolled black and white students of both sexes. Throughout the North and the Midwest, blacks organized musical groups of all descriptions, from brass bands to symphony orchestras; gaining fame, too, were such individual performers as opera singer Thomas Bowers, billed as the "Colored Mario."

Among those who earned international musical success was Elizabeth Taylor Greenfield (1809–76). Born into slavery in Natchez, Mississippi, Greenfield was bought and freed by a white Philadelphia Quaker who recognized her potential as a great singer. After several years of voice training, she began to perform across the United States and Canada. Praised by music critics for her extraordinary vocal range, Greenfield—known as the "Black Swan"—attracted the interest of Britain's Queen Victoria, who invited her to sing at Buckingham Palace in 1854.

Another outstanding musician of the day was Francis (Frank) Johnson (1792–1844). One of Amer-

Known as the "Black Swan," former Mississippi slave Elizabeth Taylor Greenfield became one of America's most admired singers. Greenfield performed all over North America as well as in England, where she gave a concert for Queen Victoria in 1854.

ica's first black bandmasters, Johnson also proved himself a superior fiddler and "society" orchestra leader. Music fans hailed him as the nation's preeminent bugler, a reputation that earned him a series of European concert tours. Like the "Black Swan," Johnson gave a command performance for Queen Victoria, who presented him with a silver bugle.

Religious music, too, provided a large field for gifted blacks. Pioneering cleric Richard Allen, who

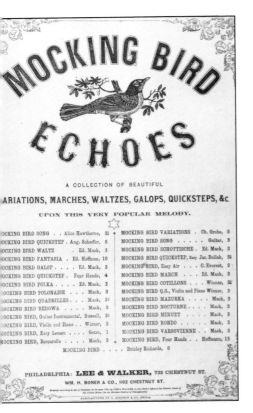

*"Listen to the Mocking Bird,"
a song written by black
composer Richard Milburn,
was so popular that it inspired
dozens of waltzes, polkas,
quicksteps, marches, and
other "echoes," or musical
pieces based on the original.
Well before the end of
American slavery, gifted
blacks proved themselves
productive and influential
in the arts and sciences.*

founded the African Methodist Episcopal (AME) Church, the first major black institution in America—and who died at the age of 71 in the year of Nat Turner's revolt—wrote the first hymn book for African Americans in 1801. By the mid-1800s, the United States boasted scores of AME congregations, many of them offering superb professional choirs, organ accompaniment for parishioners' singing, and frequent concerts of sacred music.

At another musical level—show business—blacks also gained a share of the limelight. The hit song of the 1850s, with black and white audiences alike, was "Listen to the Mocking Bird," the work of black composer Richard Milburn. And the sensation of the New York City stage was William Henry Lane, a black performer known as "Master Juba, the Greatest of All Dancers." When the celebrated British novelist Charles Dickens visited America in 1841, he headed straight for New York's world-famous "Five Points," the honky-tonk district that offered entertainment by Master Juba as well as "hot music" by African American fiddlers, drummers, and trumpeters.

But it was in the fight against slavery that blacks exerted their most concentrated efforts. This was a struggle that became more difficult with each year that followed Turner's amazing revolt. Law after law made life almost as perilous for free northern blacks as it was for slaves. Working to fight the effects of those laws were the courageous inheritors of Nat Turner's legacy: such activists as Underground Railroad "conductor" Harriet Tubman and abolitionists Frederick Douglass, William Still, and Sojourner Truth, along with countless unknown slaves and free blacks who risked their

lives for freedom. Joining in this difficult and dangerous work were a number of whites, among them the
crusading antislavery activist William Lloyd Garrison.

Through newspapers and speeches, rallies, and
acts of heroic resistance, African Americans would
join with like-minded whites to throw off the chains
of two and a half centuries. While these abolitionists
fought with words and daring acts, black warriors in
the Second Seminole War of 1835–42 would show
just how well African Americans could fight, even
against the military might of the United States.

FREEDOM'S JOURNAL.

" RIGHTEOUSNESS EXALTETH A NATION."

CORNISH & RUSSWURM, } **NEW-YORK, FRIDAY, MARCH 16, 1827.**   VOL. I. NO. 1.
Editors & Proprietors. }

2

BLOOD ON THE CORN

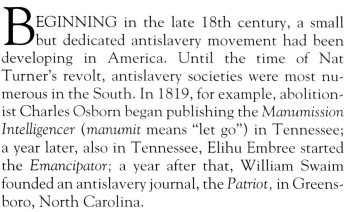

BEGINNING in the late 18th century, a small but dedicated antislavery movement had been developing in America. Until the time of Nat Turner's revolt, antislavery societies were most numerous in the South. In 1819, for example, abolitionist Charles Osborn began publishing the *Manumission Intelligencer* (*manumit* means "let go") in Tennessee; a year later, also in Tennessee, Elihu Embree started the *Emancipator*; a year after that, William Swaim founded an antislavery journal, the *Patriot*, in Greensboro, North Carolina.

Abolition societies also sprang up in Maryland, Virginia, and other southern border states. The American Colonization Society, however, attracted thousands of members on both sides of the Mason-Dixon Line. (Named for Charles Mason and Jeremiah Dixon, British surveyors who mapped the area in 1767, the line ran from Maryland to Pennsylvania, marking the invisible but very real boundary between the North and the South.)

The first issue of Freedom's Journal *on March 16, 1827, carried the black newspaper's biblical slogan, "Righteousness Exalteth a Nation." The Reverend Samuel Cornish (left) and journalist John Brown Russwurm (right) founded the paper together, but they separated over the issue of colonization, which Russwurm favored and Cornish opposed.*

THE EMANCIPATOR.

VOL. I.]   JONESBOROUGH, APRIL 30, 1820.   [NO. 1.

EDITED AND PUBLISHED BY ELIHU EMBREE, AT $1 PER ANNUM—IN ADVANCE.

ADDRESS,
OF THE EDITOR.

The EMANCIPATOR will be published monthly in *Jonesborough*, Ten. by *E L I-H U E M B R E E*, on a fine superroyal sheet of paper, in octava form, at *One Dollar* per annum, payable on receipt of the first number.

This paper is especially designed by the editor to advocate the abolition of slavery, and to be a repository of tracts on that interesting and important subject. It will contain all the necessary information that the editor can obtain of the progress of the abolition of the slavery of the descendants of Africa; together with a concise history of their introduction into slavery, collected from the best authorities.

The constitutions and proceedings of the several benevolent societies in the United States and elsewhere who have had this grand object in view, will be carefully selected and published in the Emancipator.

A correspondence between those societies, and between individuals in different parts of the nation on the subject of emancipation, will be kept up through the medium of this paper by inserting in its pages all interesting communications, letters, &c. that may come to the knowledge of the editor.

The speeches of those have been and are eminently advocating this glorious cause, either in the congress of the U. S. the state legislatures, or in the parliaments and courts of other nations, will be strictly attended to.

Biographical sketches of the lives of those who have been eminent in this cause, will also occasionally find a place in this work.

A portion of this paper is intended to be devoted as a history of the abolition of the African slave trade, in every part of the world, from its first dawn, down to the present times.

In the prosecution of this work the editor professes that he expects (like other periodical editors) to live much upon the borrow; and to make use of such materials as he may find in his way, suited to his object, without being very particular to take up much time or room in acknowledging a loan, unless he may think it necessary, willing that others should use the same freedom with him, & hoping that by offering such a fair exchange, such borrowing will be thought no robbery.

Communications on the subject, and materials for the work are solicited and will be thankfully received both from societies and individuals friendly to the abolition of slavery. Such communications, if approved of by the editor, will find a harty welcome in the *Emancipator.*

The Manumission Society of Tenn. in particular, it is expected will afford many tracts on the subject of slavery, which the editor assures them he will feel inclined to respect; and where his judgment should not otherwise dictate, will give them an early and gratuitous insertion. They will find in the Emancipator a true chronicle of the proceedings of that benevolent society as far as the editor is enabled—And for this purpose the clerks of the conventions, and of each branch of the society are requested to forward from time to time true copies of all their minutes, which may not be really improper to publish (and it is hoped there will be none such) together with the names of their members, their places of residence, &c. all which particulars we are of opinion will not be unprofitable to the cause of abolition to be published.

Letters from one individual to another, with the names of both, we think will be often beneficial to be published. If they do nothing more they will shew that all are not asleep nor dumb to the cries of suffering humanity.

Those who have had, or may have law suits on hand for the freedom of such as are unlawfully held in bondage, are desired to forward the true history of the facts, their progress, final decision, &c. with the places of residence and names of plaintiff's and defendant's, with eve-

White Tennessean Elihu Embree started publishing an antislavery newspaper, the Emancipator, *in 1820. Contrary to popular belief, some of the nation's strongest abolitionist views came from the heart of the slaveholding South.*

Established in 1817, the American Colonization Society aimed to free America's slaves and "colonize" them in their ancestral homeland. To this end, the colonizationists, as the society's members called themselves, bought land on the west coast of Africa. There they created the black republic of Liberia, named from the Latin word *liber*—"free." The society's money came both from private donations and state treasuries, such as those of Virginia and Maryland. But although the colonizationists raised large sums and worked doggedly, they could not keep up with history. By the 1830s, blacks were being born into American slavery at a faster rate than freed blacks could be transported to Africa.

The American Colonization Society also faced distrust within its own ranks. Northern members began to suspect—perhaps rightly—that their southern colleagues were working against the common cause. According to these suspicions, the southerners had more interest in strengthening slavery by shipping potentially disruptive free blacks out of the country than in encouraging slaveholders to free their human chattel. Colonization continued to receive some support, but by about 1840 most of its efforts had ceased to bear much fruit. Other branches of the antislavery movement, however, were blossoming.

In 1827 John B. Russwurm and Samuel E. Cornish began publishing *Freedom's Journal*, the first black

White officials of the American Colonization Society force "nuisances"—freed slaves—onto a Liberia-bound ship in this satirical 1839 cartoon. Opponents of colonization maintained that the back-to-Africa scheme was nothing but a ruse for ridding the South of troublesome free blacks.

1839.]   *Anti-Slavery Almanac.*   29

FOR LIBERIA

" NUISANCES " GOING AS " MISSIONARIES," " WITH THEIR OWN CONSENT."

newspaper in the United States. Russwurm was one of the nation's first two black college graduates, and Cornish, also black, was a respected Presbyterian minister. Their publication denounced slavery with the stunning clarity of Thomas Jefferson's "firebell in the night." By 1829 another voice had joined those of Russwurm and Cornish; this one belonged to David Walker, a free black who, two years before Nat Turner's revolt, published a pamphlet entitled "Walker's Appeal in Four Articles Together with a Preamble to the Colored Citizens of the World But in Particular, and very Expressly, to those of the United States of America." Walker's meaning was unmistakable: "I ask you . . . are we MEN?" he thundered. "America is more our country than it is the whites'— we have enriched it with our *blood and tears*." Walker's demand, that blacks should rise up against their masters, naturally sent chills of terror through the South.

Ever since Gabriel Prosser's revolt, attempted in the year Nat Turner was born, nervous whites had watched the sky for the glow of burning barns. (Prosser, a Virginia slave, organized a massive revolt to free all the blacks in the state; two informers told their masters about the conspiracy, leading to the capture and execution of Prosser and his lieutenants.) In 1822, a more nearly successful rebellion had been staged in Charleston, South Carolina. Planned by Denmark Vesey, an educated former slave who had bought his own freedom in 1800, this uprising involved hundreds, perhaps even thousands, of blacks. Vesey had encouraged his followers with highly inflammatory words—"We hold . . . that all men are created equal, that they are endowed by their Creator with certain inalienable Rights, that among these are Life, Liberty, and the Pursuit of Happiness . . ."—from the nation's own Declaration of Independence. Vesey was hanged along with 35 of his allies.

To counteract the fears raised by such black rebels as Prosser, Vesey, Walker, Cornish, and Russwurm, Virginia and other southern states began to mobilize militias on an awesome scale. There were, in theory, 101,488 civilian soldiers in place by the time of Turner's revolt; 10 percent of Virginia's population was ready to defend the state in the event of a slave uprising. Each company of militia was a living symbol of the South's two-edged thinking. On one edge, southerners claimed to believe their slaves were happy with their lot; on the other, the whites were making active preparations for a revolt they seemed to feel could happen at any moment.

Slaveholders had felt deep anxiety before 1831, but Turner's revolt would fill them with unbounded terror and rage. The son of slaves, Turner was born near the small community of Jerusalem, Virginia, on October 2, 1800; this was also the birth year of John Brown, the fiery white abolitionist who would lead his own bloody insurrection in 1859.

Turner's character was formed in Virginia's Southampton County, a once-tranquil corner of the "Old Dominion." Southampton was marked by rolling, densely forested hills and small farms carved from the deep woods. Most of these spreads consisted of a simple rectangular main house flanked by a scattering of sheds, slave quarters, and outbuildings. Usually planted nearby was one of the apple orchards that provided Southampton's celebrated and powerful apple brandy.

About two-thirds of Southampton County's white families kept slaves, but few owned more than 10. The high proportion of blacks to whites—six to four in

1830—made Southampton a typical southern county. It was, however, distinguished from much of the Deep South by its attitude toward slavery. Here in southeastern Virginia, whites took pride in their "enlightened" treatment of blacks. Like most Virginian slaveholders, Southamptoners withheld the lash, believing that captive blacks could be better controlled through tolerance and mutual understanding. This meant slaves could visit each other on Sundays, hold church meetings and barbecues, and even go hunting or fishing when they had the time. Whites believed that in Southampton County, slaves lived contentedly under their masters' benevolent authority.

In the first 12 years of his life Turner enjoyed relative freedom, playing with friends and with the master's children—as young blacks were expected to do—while his parents worked in the fields. But Turner showed early signs that he was no ordinary child. He talked convincingly of events that had taken place before he was born, and he carried odd marks on his chest and head—signs, according to African lore, of a prophet. He showed other remarkable qualities, too: he learned to read, apparently with no outside help. Soon even the whites noticed his sharp mind; many asserted that he was too smart to be raised a slave and that if he was, he would be of little use. Gradually, other blacks came to regard him as a leader.

Turner's early years were shaped both by religion and by his white masters. Benjamin Turner, his first owner, embraced Methodism, an evangelical, or "Gospel spreading," Protestant religion that swept Virginia in the early 19th century. Because Benjamin Turner believed that all human beings had to be "saved from Satan," he allowed all his slaves, including young Turner, to attend church meetings. There, the preachers talked of the Jews' captivity in Egypt and of the punishment that lay in store for sinners. The Day of Judgment was close, they said; the sky would

grow dark and the land be devoured by flames as punishment for the people's sins. Such sermons inspired more than a few whites to change their ways. But for blacks they contained a special message: God, in all his power and glory, was on their side.

Young Turner absorbed every word, and soon became a preacher himself. At black prayer meetings held in barns and clearings, slaves could finally enjoy some release. Services were stirring, almost magical events in which believers punctuated songs and sermons with cries of "Hallelujah!" and "Say it!" Worshipers swayed and writhed as the strong mix of African folklore and Christianity unleashed lifetimes of

Joined by their owner and his family, plantation hands listen to a fellow slave preach. Nat Turner's first master and other "enlightened" slaveholders encouraged their people to attend church services, but stopped when they recognized the Bible as a potential inspiration for revolt.

Nat Turner (pointing) rehearses his men for the Southampton County, Virginia, uprising of August 22, 1831. The revolt claimed some 200 lives and pushed the nation closer to the great civil war that would engulf it 30 years later.

pent-up emotion. Church was a place, as one black reportedly said, to be "free indeed, free from death, free from hell, free from work, free from white folks, free from everything."

Rubbed raw by the yoke of slavery, Turner began to see visions. Once, he later said, he looked skyward and beheld "white spirits and black spirits engaged in battle." The sun had been "darkened—the thunder

rolled in the Heavens, and blood flowed in the streams." Turner also saw "signs": blood on the corn and leaves etched in blood—pictures of men in combat. Finally, on August 22, 1831, he turned his visions into action, assembling his small band and giving them their orders: after striking at the Travis house, they would go on to kill all the white masters. By the time the rebels had seized the armory in nearby Jerusalem, Turner asserted, the slaves of Southampton and its surrounding counties would rise up and join them. Soon they would all be free—or dead.

The men finished off the Travises, took the family's weapons, and struck out for the Turner farm. After hacking down every visible white man, woman, and child, they gathered more weapons and new slave recruits, then went on to repeat the performance at the next farm. By Monday morning, Turner's men had cut an awesome swath of destruction, devastating 15 homesteads and killing more than 50 whites. Turner now divided his 80 men into two groups, one mounted, the other walking. Streaking ahead, the riders would accomplish most of the killing before Turner, who rode between the two columns, even arrived. In the entire revolt, Turner personally committed only one of the approximately 60 murders.

Meanwhile, rumors were shooting around the county like an electric current. Something horrible was going on in Southampton! White militiamen soon spread out across the countryside, often stumbling upon the rebels' work before the blood had dried. Armed mainly with axes and antique muskets, the rebels were no match for the well-equipped militias; within a week whites had rounded up most of Turner's men and taken them to Jerusalem. Turner himself, however, remained at large.

For days the area bristled with armed white men roaming the countryside and firing at every black in sight. As the planters mopped up the rebellion, they butchered as many as 120 innocent blacks. Nat Turner held out for six weeks, hiding in a cave not far from the Travis farm where the revolt had begun. In the end, he was discovered almost by accident, when a white farmer happened by his hiding place just as the fugitive poked his head out. Realizing that there was no escape, Turner surrendered quietly. The revolt was over.

On November 5, 1831, Turner's captors led him in irons to face his prosecutors at the county courthouse in Jerusalem. By this time all but a few of the other rebels had been found and tried—or lynched. Of the approximately 50 who stood trial, 17 went to the gallows. The rest suffered lesser penalties, most often deportation, which meant being sold into the Deep South to work on the massive plantations there.

Turner faced the hushed courtroom calmly, his hands weighed down by chains but his head up. Coolly engaging the eyes of the judge, Jeremiah Cobb, he said he felt no guilt for what he had done. He also admitted to instigating the revolt. The court clerk then read the "full, free, and voluntary" confession that Turner had made in his jail cell several days earlier. It was a startlingly eloquent and straightforward account, not only of the revolt's savage details but of Turner's youth and the religious inspiration that shaped his thinking. When the jailer asked him if he was sorry for what he had done, now that he would certainly hang for it, Turner replied: "Was not Christ crucified?"

Turner's trial was a kind of demonstration; southerners wanted the world to know that they were fair and impartial in these matters. They assigned lawyers to Turner and the other captured slaves, and kept meticulous records of their trials. Turner's own attorney conducted his client's defense fairly and followed all his instructions, even entering his "Not Guilty" plea, which must have been difficult for the white lawyer to understand. After all the witnesses had been heard, Judge Cobb asked the defendant, "Have you anything to say why the sentence of death should not be pronounced upon you?" "Nothing but what I've said before," Turner said. After a long speech dwelling on the horrors of the revolt and Turner's guilt, Cobb crashed down his gavel and turned to the rebellious slave. "You," he said, will "be hung by the neck until you are dead! dead! dead! and may the Lord have mercy on your soul." Then the judge ordered the county to reimburse Turner's owner for his value: $375.

On November 11 officials took Turner from his cell and brought him to the "hanging tree" of Southampton County. A fascinated crowd looked on as the executioner tightened the heavy rope around the prisoner's neck. When asked if he had any last words, Turner simply said, "I am ready." Hanged moments later, he remained motionless. "Not a limb or a muscle was observed to move," said one awed witness. Turner had maintained the dignity of a prophet to the very last.

But Turner's story did not end there; in fact, the true impact of his life's work had just begun. And the final result would be very nearly as terrible and complete as his apocalyptic imaginings—precisely as his visions of "blood on the corn" had seemed to foretell. In the months that followed his execution, whites became more systematic in their efforts to control blacks. Southern laws had already prohibited the education of slaves and banned most slave meetings; now the South began to enforce those laws rigidly, to tighten security, and to mete out harsher punishments

Southampton's "hanging tree" (photographed 60 years after Turner's death) was the site of the black rebel leader's execution on November 11, 1831. Turner's only last words were the stoic and dignified "I am ready."

for black disobedience. New rules even regulated slaves' music; singing the popular spiritual "Go Down, Moses," for example, became a criminal act because the song contained such lines as, "Tell ol' Pharaoh, to let my people go."

Free blacks, too, became the focus of post-Turner southern fears. In many states, officials forced these people to leave their homes and move elsewhere. Those who balked faced lynching. To jittery whites, free black men and women posed a threat to white security, especially when the blacks tried to set up

their own schools. After all, whites reasoned, Turner
had been able to read, and look where that had
led! Furthermore, free blacks in the cities lived in their
own neighborhoods, dark and secret places where
runaway slaves might be sheltered and rebellions
planned. Many free blacks were seized and enslaved
as white anxiety swept the South.

In one sense, Turner's revolt ended in failure; he
and his allies lost their lives, and other blacks suffered
the backlash of white rage produced by his actions.
But in another sense, the revolt was one of black
history's gleaming milestones. Whites had long insisted that blacks deserved to be enslaved because they
could not—or would not—defend their freedom. This
proposition had been so often made that many blacks
saw it as a dismal truth. Turner blew that argument to
pieces. He made a mighty plan, raised and led an army,
and gave millions of blacks, most of them then un-
born, the courage to fight for racial justice and human
freedom. As historian Terry Bisson has noted:

> In black folklore, "The Second War" is a phrase that is often
> used to refer to the Civil War, a bloody struggle that put an
> end to slavery in America. "The First War" was the rebellion
> led by Nat Turner.

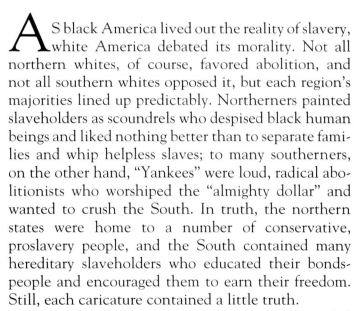

3

WAY DOWN IN
EGYPT LAND

AS black America lived out the reality of slavery, white America debated its morality. Not all northern whites, of course, favored abolition, and not all southern whites opposed it, but each region's majorities lined up predictably. Northerners painted slaveholders as scoundrels who despised black human beings and liked nothing better than to separate families and whip helpless slaves; to many southerners, on the other hand, "Yankees" were loud, radical abolitionists who worshiped the "almighty dollar" and wanted to crush the South. In truth, the northern states were home to a number of conservative, proslavery people, and the South contained many hereditary slaveholders who educated their bondspeople and encouraged them to earn their freedom. Still, each caricature contained a little truth.

Many slaveholders *were* cruel, and many regarded black people as less than human. Southerners liked to

Guided by a plantation slave, oxen haul the day's cotton harvest in this mid-19th-century oil painting. By 1850 the U.S. population included some 3.2 million enslaved African Americans.

A much-reprinted lithograph, entitled "The Old Plantation Home," presents the South's idealized view of slavery: happy "darkies" singing and dancing their days away.

picture their slaves as childlike and irresponsible, but at the same time loyal and affectionate toward their "massas." In this image, "the happy darkies" danced and laughed their days away. Many years after the Civil War, John Little, a former slave who served on a Deep South plantation, talked to an interviewer about the "carefree" life of a slave:

> They say slaves are happy, because they laugh, and are merry. I myself and three or four others, have received two hundred lashes in the day, had our feet in fetters; yet, at

night, we would sing and dance, and make others laugh at the rattling of our chains. . . . We did it to keep down trouble, and to keep our hearts from being completely broken: that is as true as the gospel! . . . I have cut capers in chains.

In the South of 1850, most whites—about three-quarters of the population—owned no slaves. Nevertheless, the whole South was dominated by the slave system. Explaining this apparent contradiction, black historian John Hope Franklin notes that most of the South's wealth came from its slave-worked plantations, "thus giving the owners an influence out of proportion to their numbers." Furthermore, according to Franklin, because most nonslaveholding southerners hoped one day to own slaves themselves, "they took on the habits and patterns of thought of the slaveholders."

Estimated at some 3.2 million in 1850, America's slave population was increasing rapidly. (By 1860 it would be almost 4 million.) In 1850 as many as 400,000 slaves lived in cities and towns, and about 1 million worked on small farms, in most cases alongside their owners—a few of whom were blacks themselves. Black planter Benjamin O. Taylor of Virginia, for example, lived in his own "Big House" and kept 71 slaves; in Louisiana, black plantation owners Cyprian Richard, Charles Rogues, and Marie Metoyer kept an average of 65 slaves apiece. Few farmers of any color, however, owned more than 20 slaves each. The remainder of the slaves—about 1.8 million people—resided on plantations, large farms whose proprietors kept as many as 1,000 slaves. These wealthy planters raised cotton, tobacco, rice, or sugarcane.

A pair of southern vigilantes—self-styled lawmen—prepare to punish a free black man for lacking a pass in 1817. Such incidents multiplied after the 1831 Turner revolt, which fanned racial fears and suspicions into a deadly blaze.

Each southern state had its own slave codes, or laws to deal with slaves, but there was little difference from one state to the next. All the codes aimed to protect whites against blacks. They all regarded slaves as property, not people, and they all concentrated on keeping the slaves from gaining any degree of independence. An independent-minded slave, the reasoning went, was not an efficient piece of property. In general, the slave codes decreed that slaves could not leave their plantations without their master's permission, and that no slave could possess a gun, make a contract, own property, or strike a white person, even in self-defense. Although masters could kill a slave without encountering much trouble from the law, few did; slaves represented a cash investment.

A wave of harsh repression followed Turner's 1831

revolt. Slaves and free blacks alike were lynched, flogged, and hounded from their homes, sometimes on the slightest whiff of suspicion. After the Turner revolt, whipping became more common, and it was used for a wider list of infractions than ever before. A slave could be whipped for learning to read, working too slowly, stealing, saying he was free, getting drunk, talking back to a white person—in short, for anything a master chose to punish him for. William Wells Brown, a former slave, said that at his plantation the whip was used "very frequently and freely, and a small offense on the part of a slave furnished an occasion for its use."

Abolitionist lecturer Frederick Douglass, himself a former slave, gave an even more specific account of southern crimes and punishments: "If more than seven slaves together are found in any road without a white person, [they get] 20 lashes apiece," he told white audiences. "For letting loose a boat where it is made fast, 30 lashes for the first offense; and for the second shall have cut off from his head one ear. For hunting with dogs in the woods, 30 lashes."

Other reasons for flogging included "impudence," described by Douglass as "almost anything, or nothing at all, just according to the caprice of the master or overseer, at the moment." This offense, he said, "may be committed in various ways; in the tone of an answer; in answering at all; in not answering; in the expression of the countenance; in the motion of the head; in the gait, manner and bearing of the slave." In Virginia, continued Douglass, whites could be executed for 3 crimes, but the laws named 71 offenses for which the life of a black could be taken.

Slaves operate a cotton gin, a machine that removes seeds from the fluffy part of the cotton boll. Eli Whitney's 1793 invention of the gin (the word is short for "engine") made cotton a highly profitable crop and vastly increased the South's demand for slave labor.

Punishments were generally administered by the plantation's overseer, a man employed by the owner to see that the slaves worked as hard and efficiently as possible. Sometimes the overseer was assisted by a driver, a slave who transmitted his leader's orders to the other slaves. Drivers, who often acted as spies on their fellow slaves, were responsible for keeping them from idling or doing poor work, and for punishing those who did. Not surprisingly, they were universally despised by their peers.

The screws had tightened, but slave life in the 1840s otherwise remained much as it had always been. A slave's life was shaped by a number of factors, including famil.. s, the location of his or her m: e characters of the owner and ov. d the majority of slave lives was none of these elements; it was King Cotton. In the years following the 1793 invention of the cotton "gin" (short for "engine"), the money-making potential of cotton production had changed the role of slaves forever.

Before the gin, separation of seeds from harvested cotton bolls was an extremely tedious, labor-intensive process; afterward, a relatively small number of slaves could process massive amounts of cotton. And the more slaves available to plant and pick this cotton, the more profit a master could make. To hundreds of southern plantation owners, it seemed financially sensible to grow one main crop, and to grow it on the largest scale possible.

Cotton was not the Deep South's only important agricultural product. Also plentiful were sugar and tobacco spreads and rice plantations, their broiling, swampy fields a hellish place to work. Most plantations also made room for corn and other food crops. But cotton dominated. It was planted—by young men and women, by old people, by children as young as six—in late March or early April.

A slave's workday began early. Just as on Nat Turner's farm in Virginia, slaves in the Deep South rose before the sun, ate a hasty meal of cold cornmeal mush, fed the farm animals, and, when they heard the sound of a horn, headed for the field. Harvesting, the most grueling work period of all on a cotton plantation, began in August and could go on until after Christmas, sometimes even into February. Cotton-picking would take place "from cain't see to cain't see," as the slaves described the time between dawn and dusk.

Working in fields that stretch to the horizon, slaves pick cotton in Georgia. By 1834, the southern "Cotton Kingdom" was producing some half-billion pounds of cotton each year, almost all of it planted, harvested, and processed by African American labor.

When darkness halted their picking, the slaves turned to ginning. In the time between the two jobs, there was a host of heavy chores: land to clear, kindling to split, chickens to kill, water to haul, equipment to repair, underbrush to burn, fences to mend, fertilizer to spread. Only after they finished all their work could the slaves pause for their evening meal. Afterward, usually at around 10 P.M., the horn sounded again, telling those in the quarters to get to bed for the few hours until dawn. At the end of the cotton season, the slaves turned to harvesting and shucking corn, another job that could go on until the early hours of the morning. On plantations whose

main crop was sugar, the harvest season meant even more serious toil; the sugar mills ran all night, and slaves often worked 18 to 20 hours at a stretch.

The conditions to which slaves returned at the end of their workday were determined by the master. Almost all plantation slaves lived in small log huts, few of which boasted windows, wooden floors, or furniture. Most of these rough cabins sheltered seven to ten people, usually members of a family. Occasionally, 30 or so slaves might inhabit a single long, low shed. For bedding, cabin occupants used straw or corn husks laid over the dirt floor and a single blanket—essential, even in the Deep South, to fend off the wind that whistled through the unchinked cracks. When visitors from abroad questioned the slaves' wretched accommodations, masters were likely to reply that houses were unimportant to slaves, as they spent so little time in them. Here, at least, the slaveholder had a point; by the time they finished a day's work, slaves probably felt too exhausted to care where they ate or slept.

Some owners, of course, were more generous than others, providing slaves with gardens, warm clothes, and rudimentary medical services. Others cared less for their slaves' comfort and health. Generally, masters made a specific allotment of food that each slave would receive every day, but their notion of what was enough to keep a single person healthy varied sharply. The average weekly supply for an adult was about three pounds of salt pork and one peck of flour or cornmeal. Sometimes this basic ration was improved by the addition of fruit, sweet potatoes, rice, or corn syrup. Most former slaves told of at least one master who provided too little food. To cope with this, slaves raised crops if they were allowed to and stole it if they were not.

Some plantations allowed weekend barbecues, and most whites set aside certain times, such as Christmas, as slave holidays. Some southern state laws required owners to give their slaves Sundays off, and bad weather could also lead to a respite from work. These occasions provided opportunities for African American culture to assert itself in singing, dancing, cooking, and storytelling.

Important as work breaks were for the slaves, they also served a valuable purpose for slave owners. "I believe," wrote Frederick Douglass, "those holidays were among the most effective means in the hands of slaveholders of keeping down the spirit of insurrection among the slaves. But for these, the rigors of bondage would have been too severe for endurance, and the slaves would have been forced into a dangerous desperation."

Domestic slaves, who labored in the Big House and directly saw to the needs of the owner and his family, were in a class by themselves. They generally dwelled in or near the plantation's main house, and lived in considerably more comfort than slaves in the "quarters." The domestics were better off than the field hands in some ways—they wore better clothes, performed lighter tasks, and ate tastier food—but some aspects of their lives were even harder to bear. They were constantly under the scrutiny of their masters and mistresses, and they were required to behave with submissiveness and docility. A field hand might have to bow his head, shuffle his feet, and pretend deference once in a while, but domestic servants were expected to act as though they enjoyed their work and genuinely liked their white owners, families, and friends.

The Big House thus became a psychological battlefield, in which whites realized daily their depend-

Painted around 1800, this rare slave portrait depicts Nancy Fort, a Georgia domestic worker. In some ways, a house slave's job was easier than field labor, but it involved oppressively close scrutiny by whites.

ence on the blacks who prepared their food and ensured their comforts, and blacks just as regularly came face to face with the whites' absolute authority over them. Masters, who wanted to believe their slaves felt a childlike devotion to them, encouraged an illusion of mutual love and loyalty; slaves, who simply wanted their lives to be no worse than they had to be, often helped maintain that illusion.

A slave auctioneer takes bids on a woman, offered for sale with or without her daughter. Although some owners made an effort to keep families together, others regarded their slaves simply as property, heedlessly separating husbands from wives and children from parents.

The master might set the limits within which a slave had to live, but the slave's personal life was governed by his or her family. Relationships within an old, extended family created a special place for the slave—a world that was controllable within one that was not. The black family offered a sense of permanence, and although it was always threatened by the possibility that any of its members could be sold at any time, enormous value was put on whatever familial links a person could maintain.

Forming and keeping a family intact, however, was no simple matter for the slave. Marriages between slaves had no legal basis in the white world, and husbands, wives, and children could be, and often were, sold as individuals. In many cases, the master would decide which people married. After he had

selected a black man's bride, recalled Charles Grandy, a former slave in Virginia, "he would lead you and de woman over to one of the cabins and stand you on de porch. . . . He'd stand right dere at de do' and open de Bible . . . and read somethin' real fast out of it. Den he close up de Bible an' finish up wid dis verse:

> Dat yo' wife
> Dat yo' husban'
> I'se yo' marsa
> She yo' missus
> You married."

Often it was the occasion of a slave sale that brought out the true depth of emotional attachment among black family members. A number of wrenching accounts describe both the sorrow of forcibly parted family members and the persistent sense of family connection, even among people who knew they would never meet again. When Abream Scriven was sold by his master, he wrote his wife: "Give my love to my father and mother and tell them good Buy for me, and if we Shall not meet in this world, I hope to meet in heaven."

Together with family life, religion played a major role in slaves' lives. If a given master was particularly religious, he might see that his slaves had regular instruction from a white minister. Even the Gospel, however, was used to reinforce white control; a favorite verse of the clergymen was Ephesians 6:5: "Servants, be obedient to them that are your masters." Teaching religion was sharply curtailed after the Turner revolt, as the Methodism that so affected Turner's life was seen as a major inspiration of the insurrection. Although many slaves became deeply devout Christians, others felt the same contempt for the white man's faith as they felt for the white man himself. One northern visitor to the South recalled hearing a "prayer" coming from a black cabin, then listening with astonishment to its words:

Our father, who is in heaven
White man owe me eleven, and pay me seven,
Thy kingdom come, thy will be done,
And if I hadn't took that, I wouldn't have none.

Slaves who accepted Christianity found great comfort in it. To these abused people, a god who delivered the Israelites from bondage would surely rescue them. "Didn't my Lord deliver Daniel," they sang, "and why not every man." Over the years, the rhythms and folklore of West Africa melded with biblical themes and images. From old African work songs, in which one singer would call out a verse and the workers would respond in unison, there grew the "negro spiritual." And blacks often adapted Christian hymns to their own lives; a favorite was "I'm gonna tell God all my troubles/when I get home . . . I'm gonna tell him the road was rocky/when I get home. . . ."

Religion, rigid slave codes, and the lash kept slaves "in their place" to a certain degree. But the captured Africans and their descendants were men and women of real flesh and blood, and few had any use for their so-called place. Historian Kenneth M. Stampp (in his 1956 book, *The Peculiar Institution*) describes the situation this way:

> The record of slave resistance forms a chapter in the story of the endless struggle to give dignity to human life. Though the history of southern bondage reveals that men *can* be enslaved under certain conditions, it also demonstrates that their love of freedom is hard to crush. The subtle expressions of this spirit, no less than the daring thrusts for liberty, comprise one of the richest gifts the slaves have left to posterity.

Slaves had some influence on their treatment; because they vastly outnumbered their masters, especially on the plantations of the Deep South, their silent unity could instill a certain respect. Through passive resistance—pretending not to understand a particular task, slowing down on the job, feigning

illness, "accidentally" breaking tools or setting fires—slaves gained a measure of control over their masters and their own lives.

But not all resistance was passive. Countless revolts, attempted, defeated, and unrecorded, took place across the pre–Civil War South. Sometimes slaves rebelled by injuring or even destroying their master's most valuable property—themselves. Sui-

Louisiana slaves hold a service for one of their departed number. Religion played an important role in the lives of the captured Africans; God, they reasoned, rescued the Israelites from bondage, and would rescue them as well.

cide, especially among newly landed Africans, was common, and numerous slaves mutilated their own bodies to make themselves useless as workers. Historian Franklin writes of a slave carpenter in Kentucky, for example, who "cut off one of his hands and the fingers of the other when he learned that he was to be sold down the river."

Rather than do violence to themselves, some did it to others, repaying abuse with interest. Southerners did not like to talk about it, but surviving newspapers offer frequent reports of slaves killing their masters and overseers. A common weapon was poison; given intimate access to the Big House kitchens, domestic servants had plenty of opportunity to lace their masters' food with arsenic or ground glass, and they did. "Negroes," reported South Carolina's *Charleston Gazette* in 1761, "have begun the hellish act of poisoning." Any slave caught in the act of murder faced certain death, but some individuals seemed to think it was worth it. The killing of Kentucky slaveholder Carolina Turner offers a case in point.

> **Turner had become notorious, even among her slave-owning neighbors, for her merciless use of the lash. But as she was administering a brutal flogging one day, her victim suddenly rose up and strangled her. The community knew she had been inviting murder, but the slave was nevertheless sentenced to death, and all the area's blacks were ordered to attend the execution. Whites assumed they would be properly terrified by their friend's hanging—but when he mounted the gallows, they smiled and cheered instead. The scene sent chills through the white spectators, who probably never understood what they had seen.**

Contrary to popular belief, says Lerone Bennett, Jr. (in his 1962 book, *Before the Mayflower*), slaves defiantly disobeyed their owners, running away, killing themselves or their masters, committing sabotage. In fact, asserts the noted black historian, "they did all these things and more. They did them so often that it is nothing short of amazing that the myth of the docile Negro persists." Many slaves chose to run. Singly and in groups, they fled to Florida and Louisiana before these territories joined the Union, and they raced for the Canadian or Mexican border. Masters advertised for their runaways: "no marks except those on back," read the posters, or "will no doubt show the marks of a recent whipping." (Such descriptions, notes John Hope Franklin, "suggest a type of brutality that doubtless contributed toward the slave's decision to abscond.")

Some escaped slaves stayed in the South, making night raids on local plantations and finding refuge in woods and swamps. "What a life it must be!" wrote northern observer Frederick Law Olmsted in his 1861 book, *The Cotton Kingdom*, "to be constantly in dread of the approach of a white man as a thing [worse] than wildcats or serpents." Other fugitives headed north, some of them guided by the stars, some of them relying on the system known as the Underground Railroad. By the 1840s, especially in the Upper South, chances for escape from slave life were improving.

4

THE UNDERGROUND RAILROAD

ALTHOUGH all aiming for the same goal—the end of slavery—abolitionists employed a variety of methods. Some chose violence. The rebels— Turner, Prosser, Vesey, and countless others whose names will never be known—seized arms and marched squarely into battle. Outmanned and outgunned, they could not win and they knew it. But they kept coming, powered by the fierce determination of chained men longing to be free.

Other abolitionists, equally determined, fought slavery not by direct confrontation but by flight. These people built the Underground Railroad, a quiet but unstoppable movement that emerged at about the time of Turner's 1831 revolt. Not an actual system with rails and cars, the UGRR, as it was sometimes called, was an elaborate program for guiding slaves to freedom. Its "conductors" were courageous men and women who led runaway blacks, both in groups and

Captured West Africans seize the Spanish slave ship Amistad *off the coast of Cuba. News of the daring 1839 mutiny delighted abolitionists and sent a thrill of hope through the South's slave quarters.*

individually, along secret routes to the North; its "stations" were the safe houses along the way where, in defiance of the law, conductors secretly fed, sheltered, and advised runaway slaves.

As the years passed, the Underground Railroad reached deeper and deeper into the South, helping thousands of blacks escape the grip of slavery. The antislavery movement was growing steadily in both North and South, but northerners were far more open in expressing their support for it. When, for example, news of Nat Turner's revolt reached Torrington, Connecticut (hometown of fervent antislavery crusader John Brown), one elderly resident jumped to his feet and shouted, "The slaves have risen down in Virginia, and are fighting for their freedom as we did for ours. I pray God that they may get it!"

Another "Yankee," editor George Henry Evans of New York's *Daily Sentinel*, probably spoke for many of his neighbors when he wrote:

> [The Southampton rebels] no doubt thought that their only hope . . . was to put to death, indiscriminately, the whole race of those who held them in bondage. If such were their impressions, were they not justifiable in doing so? Undoubtedly they were, if freedom is the birthright of man, as the Declaration of Independence tells us. . . . Those who kept them in slavery and ignorance alone are answerable for their conduct.

Northerners also cheered an 1839 news bulletin that concerned the *Amistad*, a Spanish schooner carrying a cargo of captured West Africans to the sugar plantations of Cuba. Among these blacks was Sing-Gbe, the son of a tribal chief from what is now the Republic of Sierra Leone on the west coast of Africa. Like his fellow prisoners, the young man had been subjected to savage mistreatment during the three-month

voyage from Africa; chained below decks, the Africans were force-fed ("like geese for the market," noted one observer) and whipped into obedience. To protect their "merchandise" from infection, crew members rubbed vinegar and gunpowder into their captives' wounds.

Able to bear no more, Sing-Gbe (who became popularly known as Cinque) led a revolt when the ship reached Cuba. The Africans, by now unchained, slipped up to the deck, seized the crew's sugar-cane knives, and killed the ship's tyrannical captain and cook. The mutineers put the remaining crew members over the side in lifeboats, but they kept two navigators, whom they ordered to set course for Africa. The whites, however, tricked them, eventually bringing the *Amistad* to Long Island, New York, where it came under the guns of a U.S. Navy brig.

The U.S. government promptly charged Cinque and his men with murder and piracy, an accusation that kicked off one of the century's most sensational trials. (Some historians credit it with hastening the start of the Civil War.) The *Amistad* case finally reached the U.S. Supreme Court, where former president John Quincy Adams defended the mutineers. The Court ruled that the men were not Spanish property and must "be declared free . . . and go without delay." Covering the *Amistad* trial, a New York newspaper reporter described Cinque as displaying everything "from the cool contempt of a haughty chieftain to the high resolve which would be sustained through martyrdom. . . . Many white men might take a lesson in dignity and forbearance from the African chieftain."

> Sympathetic Americans raised money for Cinque, and in 1841, he chartered a brig and sailed all his men back to Sierra Leone. If he could relive the events of the *Amistad,* a reporter asked him many years later, would he not pray for the captain and the cook instead of killing them? Cinque answered quickly. "Yes, I would pray for 'em," he said, "and kill 'em, too!" In 1880, the 67-year-old Cinque died in his native land, a free man.

The *Amistad* trial sent shock waves through the South as well as the North. On a Maryland farm, young Harriet Ross probably heard a whispered report of the black mutineers' victory and, like other slaves across the South, rejoiced at the news. Ross belonged to Edward Brodas, a wealthy planter in the Tidewater region of the Chesapeake Bay. Born in 1820, she knew the briefest of childhoods. Brodas treated his slaves as a kind of cash crop, and when Harriet was only five he rented her out as a servant to a nearby family. Worked half to death, the little girl was returned to the Brodas plantation, where her mother nursed her back to health. When she was seven, Brodas rented her out again, and again she was returned, this time barely able to walk after a savage whipping. From then on, she split fence rails and loaded timber; it was back-breaking toil, but to Ross, preferable to working under the scrutiny of whites. She later said of her masters, "They didn't know any better, it's the way they were brought up . . . with the whip in their hand." She went on, "Now that wasn't the way on all plantations. There were good masters and mistresses, as I've heard tell. But I didn't happen to come across any of them."

In 1835 Ross refused to help her overseer punish another slave. The slave bolted, and the overseer

Frail and unassuming in appearance, Harriet Tubman was no stranger to firearms or violence. After escaping slavery in 1849, the 29-year-old Marylander strapped on a pistol, returned to the South, and led more than 300 African Americans to freedom.

hurled a heavy lead weight at him. The weight struck Ross instead, knocking her out and leaving a deep gash in her head. For the rest of her life, she would carry the scars of that encounter: a marked dent in her forehead and a propensity for sudden terrifying blackouts.

By the time rumors of the *Amistad* mutiny reached the Brodas plantation, Harriet Ross had already begun to dream of freedom. She later described one of her dreams: "I seemed to see a line, and on the other side of the line were green fields, and lovely flowers, and beautiful white ladies who stretched out their arms to me over the line, but I couldn't reach them. I always fell before I got to the line."

By 1849 Harriet Tubman was planning her escape. (She had married John Tubman, a free black, in 1844; he not only refused to help her escape but threatened to turn her in if she tried.) She knew nothing of geography. She could not read a compass, and even if she had possessed a map she would not have known how to use it. Aside from courage and intelligence, Tubman had only one asset when she plotted her run north: her father had taught her to recognize the Big Dipper, the starry constellation known to the slaves as the Drinking Gourd. The gourd's handle pointed straight to the North Star—and freedom.

Tubman set out alone. Humming "I'm bound for the Promised Land," words from an old spiritual, as she passed through the slave quarters, Tubman said a secret good-bye to her friends and family. She headed for the house of a woman who, she had heard, would shelter slaves. This home was a "station" on the Underground Railroad, the woman a "conductor." Overcoming terrible fears of betrayal, Tubman presented herself to the woman, who gave her food, kind words, and directions to the next station.

One safe house succeeded another as Tubman trudged to freedom with only the North Star and the frigid waters of the Choptank River as her guides. Finally, after a painful, 90-mile trek through swamp and woodland, dawn broke over Harriet Tubman. She had crossed the Mason-Dixon Line into Pennsylvania; she was free. Many years later Tubman said of this moment: "When I found I had crossed that line, I looked at my hands to see if I was the same person. There was such a glory over everything; the sun came like gold through the trees, and over the fields, and I felt like I was in heaven."

Tubman went straight to Philadelphia, the Pennsylvania city in which the American abolition movement had been born. "I was a stranger in a strange land," she said later, but she was no stranger to challenge. She immediately set about getting a job, landing one as a dishwasher and assistant cook in a hotel kitchen. But her real work was awaiting her on the Underground Railroad.

When Tubman had first reached the free side of "the line," she promised herself that she would go back south and free her family, no matter what the risks. "To this solemn resolution I came," she later put it. "I was free, and [my parents, brothers, and sisters] should be free also; I would make a home for them in the North, and the Lord helping me, I would bring them all there." Before she had been long in Philadelphia, Tubman began visiting the offices of the city's abolitionist Vigilance Committee. There she heard of a Maryland woman and her children who were about to be "sold south"—sent to work in the hellish conditions of a Deep South rice plantation. Tubman recognized the Maryland woman's description as that of her own sister, Mary Bowley.

To succeed in this case, a rescue effort would have to start at once; the auction that would effectively end Mary Bowley's life was only a few days off. The rescuer would have to spirit the little family out from under the very noses of the slave auctioneers. The effort, moreover, would involve a trip to Baltimore, a notoriously dangerous city for any black, free or fugitive. Every street in the Maryland capital was known to be crawling with bounty hunters—men who made their living by capturing blacks and, for a price, turning them over to the whites who claimed to own them. The committee members said there was probably not a man in the country who could manage a rescue as intricate and hazardous as this one. They may have been right. But it *was* managed—with spectacular

Members of an Underground Railroad (UGRR) team welcome fugitive slaves to the free North. An informal network of safe houses and sympathetic "conductors"—free blacks such as Harriet Tubman as well as whites—the UGRR guided countless runaways out of the South in the decades before the Civil War.

success—by a frail 30-year-old woman who could neither read nor write and who suffered from sudden, incapacitating blackouts.

Vigilance Committee members tried to argue Tubman out of going to Baltimore. It would be too dangerous, they told her. After all, she was a fugitive slave, and in that fiercely proslavery town she could be easily found out and reenslaved—or worse. Tubman refused to listen, and in the end the men let her go. She found her relatives and without a hitch whisked them up to Philadelphia and freedom. Her sister's rescue was the first of many for Tubman. Over the next few years, she would make no fewer than 19 hazardous trips south, emancipating more than 300 slaves. Soon everyone along the Underground Railroad knew her as Moses, the most wily and courageous of all the conductors on the freedom road. Some even called her "General" Tubman. "She could not read or write," remarked one contemporary admirer, "but she had military genius."

Despite her growing fame—and the large reward offered for her head—Tubman always eluded capture. Endowed with unshakable determination and iron courage, she tolerated no wavering from her passengers. The reluctant traveler would feel the hard steel of a revolver at his head and hear Tubman's rasping command: "Move or die!" All her missions resulted in safe deliveries. "I never ran my train off the track," she proudly noted years later, "and I never lost a passenger."

Harriet Tubman was a hero of her time—arguably of all time—but she was by no means alone. Thousands of men and women, both black and white, risked their fortunes and their lives to aid the South's enslaved population. "The Underground Railroad did not seem to suffer from want of operators," writes African American historian John Hope Franklin in his authoritative 1980 book, *From Slavery to Freedom: A History of Negro Americans*. "[Archivists have] catalogued more than 3,200 active workers, and there is every reason to believe that there were many more who will remain forever anonymous."

Outstanding in this throng of dedicated abolitionists was William Still, a freeborn black man from New Jersey. With the help of white clergyman James Miller McKim, Still managed the Philadelphia Vigilance Committee, which not only planned and financed the liberation of countless blacks but helped them establish themselves in the North. Still, who hoped that all blacks would eventually be freed, kept careful accounts of all the escaping slaves he helped so that families could find their missing members after

William Still, born free in New Jersey in 1821, taught himself to read and write, joined the Philadelphia Society for the Abolition of Slavery, then became chairman of that city's Vigilance Committee. Still not only aided thousands of escaped slaves but kept scrupulous records of their origins and destinations, making later reunions of relatives possible.

emancipation. His records, published in 1872 as *The Underground Rail Road*, contained a wealth of stories about escaping slaves.

One of Still's accounts dealt with Henry Brown, a slave from Richmond, Virginia, who escaped with the help of a white friend. Brown asked his ally to nail him into a wooden packing box, mark it "This Side Up," and ship it to the Vigilance Committee in Philadelphia. The friend obliged, and 26 suffocating hours later a beaming traveler—who would be ever after known as "Box" Brown—emerged singing a hymn: "I waited patiently for the Lord and He heard my prayer."

Still and others recounted many stories of flight, all of them demonstrating the ingenuity—and occasionally the humor—of the UGRR crew. Sometimes light-complected slaves masqueraded as masters; their darker-skinned friends acted as their slaves, and the whole group would travel in style—right across the Mason-Dixon Line. Sometimes women dressed as men, men as women. One white conductor even lent her baby to a black runaway so the woman could pose as the child's "mammy." (The mother reclaimed the youngster in Philadelphia.) And to inform the next conductor about the two runaways he was passing along, a Maryland stationmaster sent this innocent-sounding message: "By tomorrow evening's mail, you will receive two volumes of *The Irrepressible Conflict* bound in black. After perusal, please forward."

After a 26-hour railroad journey nailed into a wooden crate, runaway Virginia slave Henry "Box" Brown arrives at the Philadelphia Vigilance Committee office. Jubilantly welcoming the fugitive are committee officials, including James Miller McKim (far left) and William Still (second from left.)

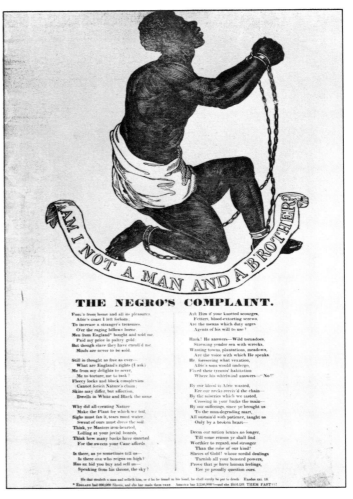

This powerful abolitionist image first appeared on a medallion made by the celebrated English potter Josiah Wedgwood in 1787. The medallion had been made at the request of American statesman and philosopher Benjamin Franklin, who said he hoped "it may have an Effect equal to that of the best written Pamphlet, in procuring Favour to these oppressed Peoples."

John Fairfield, son of a rich Virginia family, so detested slavery that he decided to move north. He took a black friend, one of his father's slaves, along with him. That success decided him to make conducting his life's work, and he made repeated forays into the South to liberate slaves. As a white man, Fairfield ran many fewer risks than Tubman, but his exploits were nonetheless impressive. During a particularly exciting escape he led 28 slaves out of bondage by putting one of them in a coffin and telling the rest to form a loudly mourning funeral procession. Fairfield died in 1860 while he was taking part in a Tennessee slave revolt.

Many of the UGRR's liberators had been enslaved themselves. John Mitchell, for example, escaped from Kentucky, enlisted in the Underground Railroad, and conducted at least 200 slaves into free territory—before being spotted by a bounty hunter, recaptured, and sold back into slavery. Mitchell, however, refused to accept defeat; he soon escaped again and took up conducting where he had left off. Another former slave, Josiah Henson, fled his master's plantation with his wife and two children and settled in Canada. Henson then taught himself to read and write, returned to Kentucky, rounded up 30 old friends and fellow slaves, and led them to Ohio and freedom.

Because the Underground Railroad operated outside the law, it kept scant records, making it impossible for modern historians to provide an exact count of the slaves who rode it to freedom. However, says John Hope Franklin, "Governor [John] Quitman of Mississippi [who governed the state from 1850 to 1851] declared that between 1810 and 1850 the South lost 100,000 slaves valued at more than $30 million." Franklin regards that figure as "fairly accurate," but whatever the figures, he adds, the Underground Railroad was "the most eloquent defiance of slaveholders that abolitionists could make."

5

"THIS SAVAGE
AND NEGRO WAR"

ALMOST as soon as the first African captives
arrived on American shores, they started trying
to escape. Most were caught and severely punished,
but every year, a few managed to break for the wilder-
ness. By the early 19th century the Deep South's rice
and cotton plantations had lost hundreds of slaves,
most of whom fled to Spanish Florida's trackless
swamps. Almost impenetrable to strangers—"dense
jungles, high grass, deadly reptiles, alligators, hordes
of insects, and tropical diseases waited for all who
entered," notes historian William Katz—this steamy
region was also rich in fish, fruit, and other food
sources, and it had fertile land for planting crops.

Much to the distress of the British and, later,
the Americans, Spain had never practiced much caution about who entered Florida. Left unmolested were
pirates, smugglers, freebooters, exiled Indians; any-
one, in short, who lived above the law—including
self-liberated Africans. The Spaniards' live-and-let-
live attitude, along with the swamps' inaccessibility

*U.S. troops battle a combined African American-Seminole
force at Okeechobee, Florida, in 1837. The skirmish was part
of the Seminole War, a long-running conflict that began when
fugitive American slaves started forging a strong alliance with
Florida's Indians.*

69

and the known combativeness of the escaped blacks, kept most slave owners from going in after their missing property. But although Florida made an ideal sanctuary for runaway slaves, the black fugitives owed their survival to the alliance they forged there. Their new allies were the Seminoles, a combination of several southeastern Indian groups driven from their original homes by European settlers. As they came to recognize each other, blacks and Seminoles made common cause out of their persecution by whites.

Vastly outnumbering the blacks, the Seminoles at first treated them as servants. But the Indians' traditional hospitality soon prevailed, and they began to accept the newcomers as equals. Although the blacks acknowledged the Seminoles' authority, they could, and often did, intermarry with them; they lived in their own homes with their own families, and they farmed land that officially belonged to them. As early as 1816 an American traveler in the region reported on black farmers in Florida: "Their corn fields extended nearly 50 miles up the river and their numbers were daily increasing."

When attacked, blacks and Indians fought side by side. As time went on, the barriers between them seemed to vanish. This relationship puzzled and angered whites. As historian Katz points out, the blacks "owned horses, cattle, hogs, and chickens and tended their own gardens. Worse, they were treated as kindly as family members—which they often were." When U.S. officials tried to persuade Seminole leaders to turn blacks in as runaways, the Seminoles insisted that they "owned" the blacks themselves. U.S. general Edmund P. Gaines at one point approached a Seminole chief on the subject. "You harbor a great many of my black people among you," said the officer. "I harbor no negroes," responded the Indian leader, "[and] I shall use force to stop any armed Americans from passing my towns or on my lands."

Another exasperated U.S. official, Indian Agent Wiley Thompson, reported that in Florida, blacks "had equal liberty with their owners." They not only traveled freely and carried firearms, he added, but acted "impudently" free.

In 1816, annoyed by Spain's refusal to capture and return escaped slaves in Florida, the U.S. government sent troops into the territory, which one army officer

Known as Negro Abraham, this former slave rose to a position of power within the Seminole culture. An on-the-spot observer said "he dictated to those of his own color, who to a great degree controlled their masters."

called "a perpetual harbor for our slaves." During this illegal invasion, a massive American force searched out "Fort Negro," a former British base converted to a black-Seminole stronghold. The mission of the American troops, spelled out by General Andrew ("Old Hickory") Jackson, was to blow up the fort and "restore the stolen negroes . . . to their rightful owners." Behind the massive walls of Fort Negro were several hundred men, women, and children, most of them either black or of mixed black and Seminole descent. The Americans demanded the fort's surrender; its black commander responded with the deafening roar of his cannons.

> **The Seminole Wars offer a graphic demonstration of the ability of African Americans under arms to resist an opponent militarily and on equal terms. If the example is rare, the rarity comes from the conditions that prevailed over most of the South, not from lack of spirit. Southerners had long derided blacks as a people who lacked the will to fight. In Florida, however, the Americans found their fiercest opponents to be the escaped blacks, whose uncompromising militance awed even professional white soldiers. Among these whites was a seasoned Indian fighter, General Sidney Thomas Jesup, commander of U.S. forces in Florida. Of the conflict, the surprised officer said, "This is a negro and not an Indian war." Echoing his thoughts, Jackson referred to it as "this savage and negro war."**

Marcus Buck, a medical officer with the army, wrote about the attack on Fort Negro. "We were pleased with their spirited opposition," he recalled, "though they were Indians, negroes and our enemies." The fort's defenders, added the officer, were "deter-

mined never to be taken alive." They were not. The Americans fired steadily, finally landing a red-hot cannonball in the renegades' gunpowder supply. The explosion that followed killed 270 defenders and injured 64. Survivors were marched off to Georgia, where they were once again enslaved.

Fugitives share food and shelter in a Louisiana swamp. As word of the Seminole-African American alliance spread through the lower South, more and more runaway slaves headed for Florida.

Less than two years after the destruction of Fort Negro, American troops again invaded Florida, this time smashing most of the black-Indian settlements west of the Suwannee River. Weary of trying to cope with this constant unrest, Spain sold Florida to the United States for $5 million in 1819. From then on, U.S. slavecatchers had a free hand; any official or private person could cross the Florida border, capture any black or person of mixed Seminole-black ancestry, and sell that individual in the slave markets of the southern United States.

Many Americans, not all of them southerners, applauded their government's actions in Florida. But many did not. In an era before opinion polls came into use, it is impossible to estimate the number who disapproved—who hated the idea of their nation acting as slavecatcher—but it was high. Congressman Joshua Reed Giddings of Ohio perhaps best summed up this faction's feelings. Addressing the House of Representatives in 1840, he sharply criticized President Martin Van Buren's administration for its campaign against people "who had fled from the oppression of professed Christians, and sought protection of savage barbarians . . . in the swamps and everglades of Florida." This "mighty nation," said the furious congressman, had brought down its "warlike energies" on a persecuted race "for no other cause than their love of liberty." In 1842, when slaves revolted on a ship carrying them from Virginia to New Orleans, Giddings praised them for seeking freedom; outraged at his open contempt for the law, the House censured (sharply criticized) him, and he resigned. In the next election, however, Ohio voters turned out in record numbers to return the antislavery crusader to Congress.

Meanwhile, the bond between the blacks and the Seminoles, based on communal living, intermarriage, and wartime alliance, had grown steadily stronger.

Even when hard-pressed by white slave owners, the Seminoles refused to give up the blacks they sheltered. The blacks, in turn, stirred the Seminoles to resist insistent white attempts to drive them out of their homes and onto western reservations. A federal Indian-affairs agent described the situation this way in 1821:

> It will be difficult to form a prudent determination with respect to the . . . negroes, who live among the Indians. . . . They fear being again made slaves, under the American government; and will omit nothing to increase or keep alive mistrust [of the United States] among the Indians, whom they in fact govern. If it should become necessary to use force with them, it is feared the Indians would take their part.

Ever since the U.S. government's 1819 purchase of Florida, its drive to get the Indians out of the area had been growing more forceful. In 1830, Congress passed the Indian Removal Act, calling for the transfer of all Indians—forcibly, if need be—to reservations in Indian Territory (essentially, the future state of Oklahoma). Five years later, frustrated slave owners presented their case to the government, citing the great monetary value of their escaped slaves and the impossibility of recovering them without military assistance. Every single black, these southerners maintained, was somebody's property, and the Indians were preventing their rightful return. Now, with slave owners, slave traders, and would-be settlers pressuring him, Andrew Jackson—elected seventh president of the United States in 1828—sent the U.S. Army into a military quagmire.

The men marching toward that Florida swamp had plenty to fear. "Ten resolute negroes, with a knowledge of the country, are sufficient to desolate the frontier, from one extent to the other," observed one officer. "The negroes, from the commencement of the Florida war," he added, "have, for their numbers, been

As a concealed "black Indian" warrior looks on, U.S. Marines nervously navigate a treacherous Florida swamp. The Indians and blacks, who knew both the area and the techniques of guerrilla warfare, had a decided advantage over the traditionally trained federal troops.

the most formidable foe, more bloodthirsty, active, and revengeful than the Indian." The reason for the battling blacks' special intensity probably lay in the fate awaiting them if they lost: if taken alive, they would be brutally punished and sent back into slavery.

The merciless Florida swamps swallowed up one regiment after another. To the white troops, the war began to seem endless, partly because of their enemies' use of guerrilla, rather than traditional, warfare. (*Guerrilla* is Spanish for "little war"). This fighting style involves small, fast-moving units of fighters who stage sudden ambushes on more numerous but less flexible opponents. In well-executed guerrilla warfare, a limited number of defenders can resist whole armies by dashing out and fighting, then retreating before the powerful enemy has time to react and destroy them.

Waged for more than two decades, the Seminole Wars had begun to exhaust the nation. One officer wrote that "if the swamps of Florida . . . become the resort of runaways [they] might impose upon the general government a contest, quadruplicate in time and treasure than that now waged." Time and treasure finally won out, and in 1842 President Martin Van Buren conceded a stalemate. The war had cost the United States $20 million, engaged more than 30,000 soldiers, and caused the deaths of 1,500 military men as well as countless civilians. No longer would the government try to weed out slaves from Afro-Indians and Seminoles. Any blacks who agreed to depart could go in peace to Indian Territory and live as free people. Southerners loudly protested the agreement, but government negotiators stood firm. "The negroes rule the Indians," insisted General Jesup, "and it is important that they should feel themselves secure; if they should become alarmed and hold out, the war will be resumed."

The blacks and Indians agreed to the peace treaty, and the Second Seminole War was over. Its resolution, however, left the allies with mixed feelings: for the Seminoles, it meant an end to a generation of bloodletting, but it also meant giving up their homeland and accustomed way of life. For the blacks, it

Soldiers drill at Fort Brooke, a U.S. military base on Tampa Bay, in the 1830s. Although the Seminole Wars pitted the army against the Indians, the Americans were far more worried about the "Negro foe."

delivered what they had wanted in the first place: freedom. But it also closed off an escape hatch for the still-enslaved men and women of the Deep South. By 1842, most of the area had been thoroughly settled by whites, leaving few places where black fugitives could find safety and from which they could gather strength.

While war raged in Florida, the abolition move-

ment in the North had been gathering steam. By the time the war wound down, the North and South were locking horns more publicly—and more brutally—than ever before. The struggle would continue to grow in intensity, and new heroes would emerge to fight it.

6

"FREDERICK, IS GOD DEAD?"

THE North's public battle over slavery intensified in the 1840s. No longer confining themselves to newsletters and speeches, partisans argued everywhere, from New England town meetings to New York town houses. According to thousands of northerners, the country—half free and half slave—was fine as it was. Disagreeing passionately, thousands of other northerners commanded their representatives to make slavery illegal. In one year (1838–39) alone, more than two million Americans signed antislavery petitions and sent them to Congress.

Overwhelmed by this flood of demands and unwilling to devote any more of their time to the issue, southern and conservative northern U.S. congressmen enacted a law known as the "gag rule." On "all petitions, memorials, resolutions, propositions, or papers relating . . . to the subject of slavery," said the 1836 resolution, "no further action shall be taken." Although strongly opposed by abolition-minded leg-

---

Born a New York State slave about 1798, Sojourner Truth gained her freedom in 1827, then became one of the nation's most accomplished orators, abolitionists, and battlers for women's rights.

Wendell Phillips, an eloquent antislavery activist, addresses a crowd of black and white abolitionists on Boston Common in the mid-1830s. In these years, millions of northerners besieged their congressmen with petitions demanding an end to slavery.

islators, the gag rule had total support from the solid South and its allies. (Some scholars consider this episode a stain on America's history. Northern citizens, they point out, had been denied the right of petition—guaranteed by the First Amendment to the Constitution—simply because the subject of slavery antagonized the South.)

Eight years after Congress passed the gag rule, Representative John Quincy Adams—son of the nation's second president and himself president from 1825 to 1829—succeeded in getting the infamous regulation repealed. Adams's words, addressed to his

colleagues in 1844, show the depth of feeling brought out by the slavery issue.

> It perverts human reason . . . to maintain that slavery is sanctioned by the Christian religion, that slaves are happy and contented in their condition, that between master and slave there are ties of mutual attachment and affection, that the virtues of the master are refined and exalted by the degradation of the slave; while at the same time they . . . burn at the stake Negroes convicted of crimes for the terror of the example, and writhe in agonies of fear at the very mention of human rights as applicable to men of color.

In the years between passage and repeal of the gag rule, the tempers of proslavery and antislavery factions had grown steadily hotter. Relatively little violence occurred in the South, not because no one opposed slavery but because those who did feared to say so. In the North, where the antislavery movement acted openly, violence began to rise. In Canterbury, Connecticut, for example, white schoolteacher Prudence Crandall opened a "High school for young colored Ladies and Misses" in 1833. Calling black women "ladies and misses"—terms whites regarded as applying only to their own females—outraged town bigots, who harassed teacher and pupils, broke school windows, passed a law prohibiting the teaching of out-of-state blacks, and finally burned down the school. In 1837 an Alton, Illinois, mob burned the presses of 35-year-old antislavery editor Elijah Lovejoy, then shot him dead when he tried to save his property. In 1838, a howling rabble set fire to Pennsylvania Hall, the Philadelphia meeting place of the Pennsylvania Society for the Abolition of Slavery, and burned it to the ground.

When educator Prudence Crandall (pictured in 1838) established a multiracial girls' school in Canterbury, Connecticut, in 1833, local bigots responded violently. After terrorizing the schoolmistress and her pupils, a mob burned the school to the ground.

Abolitionists, both black and white, nevertheless continued their crusade. Among the many Americans who fought this dangerous battle was a tall, thin black woman with the unlikely name of Sojourner Truth. Born a slave around 1798 and raised in upstate New York, Isabella Baumfree (who changed her name to Sojourner Truth in 1843) gained her freedom when New York State abolished slavery in 1827. Soon afterward she moved to New York City, where she supported herself as a maid. A fiery speaker with a deep interest in religion, Truth began preaching the gospel at the era's popular camp meetings (religious revivals). She traveled—or "sojourned"—widely, preaching salvation to huge crowds throughout New York State and New England.

In 1843 Truth moved to what is now Florence, Massachusetts, and joined the Northampton Association of Education and Industry, a community of idealistic, reform-minded people of both races and sexes. Through this group, Truth met a number of black abolitionists, including David Ruggles, secretary of the New York Vigilance Committee (one of many groups that raised money to help escaped slaves), and former slave Frederick Douglass, perhaps the antislavery movement's most prominent member. Truth also established a strong friendship with a white man; he was William Lloyd Garrison, publisher of the abolitionist newspaper the *Liberator* and founder of the influential New England Anti-Slavery Society. Impressed with these crusaders' zeal, Truth adopted her new name and turned her preaching talents to a new subject: abolition.

Truth's experience of bondage had been brutal. In her speeches she held nothing back, expressing her hatred for slavery in terms of religious mysticism and speaking in a deep, resonant voice. When she began lecturing, few of her audiences had heard much about the realities of slavery, and fewer still had heard about them from a former slave, let alone a woman. Truth was such a powerful speaker, in fact, that some listeners refused to believe she *was* a woman. After one particularly vivid lecture, a group of antifeminist, antiblack men tried to shame her off the stage by demanding that she prove herself a female. The aging Truth hesitated for only a moment, then bared her breasts. "It's not my shame but yours," she said softly. In an era when "nice" women revealed not even a glimpse of ankle, Truth's action stunned her listeners into frozen silence, but the lecture hall soon resounded with applause for her courage. Her tormentors slunk toward the exit.

Because Truth had never learned to read or write, her articulate speech, deep convictions, and grasp of ideas sometimes astonished audiences. She also displayed uncommon wit. A characteristic moment occurred when a man in a midwestern audience jeered

Leading abolitionist William Lloyd Garrison looked meek, but he was a raging bull on human rights. Announcing in the first issue of his crusading newspaper, the Liberator, *that he would never compromise on slavery, he thundered: "I am in earnest—I will not equivocate—I will not excuse—I will not retreat a single inch—AND I WILL BE HEARD!"*

at her for using a pipe. Smoking made the breath unclean, said the man, and "the Bible tells us that no unclean thing can enter the kingdom of heaven." That might be so, Truth shot back, "but when I go to heaven I expect to leave my breath behind me."

Truth was introduced to the women's movement in the 1840s, but she found it baffling at first. After listening to speeches by the great rights crusaders Elizabeth Cady Stanton and Lucy Stone at a convention, she said, "Sisters, I ain't clear what you'd be after. If women want any rights more than they's got, why don't they just take them, and not be talking about it?" But when she came to understand the vast legal inequality facing the women of her day—they were not allowed to vote or own property, had no rights to their own children, few opportunities to get an education, and almost none of entering a profession—Truth became a star of the women's movement as well as the abolitionists'. The former slave continued to speak for black freedom, but as time went on she put equal emphasis on *female* freedom. The two could not be separated, she insisted. "If colored men get their rights, and not colored women," she told audiences, "colored men will be masters over the women, and it will be just as bad as before."

Courageous and outspoken, Sojourner Truth was particularly celebrated for her speed and sharpness in debate. On one occasion—an 1852 women's rights convention in Akron, Ohio—for example, she heard a clergyman say women should never have the vote because they were "weak." Wiry and imposing—she stood more than six feet tall—Truth took the podium. What did the minister mean by "weak"? No man had ever helped *her* into a carriage or over a mud puddle! Then raising her voice, she said, "And ain't I a woman? Look at me! Look at my arm!" She rolled her sleeve to the shoulder. "I have plowed, and planted, and gathered into barns, and no man could head me. And ain't I a woman? I could work as much and eat as much as a man—when I could get it—and bear the lash as well! And ain't I a woman?" Now Truth's voice rose to a thunderous pitch. "I have borne 13 children, and seen 'em most all sold off to slavery, and when I cried out with my mother's grief, none but Jesus heard me! And ain't I a woman?"

That show-stopping speech was capped by Truth's rebuttal to another clergyman, this one insisting that men should rule the world because Jesus Christ had been a man. Truth made short work of that argument: "Where did your Christ come from?" she asked him. He remained silent, so she answered for him. "From God and a woman," she snapped. "Man had nothing to do with Him."

Another moment of Truth came during a lecture by Frederick Douglass. The silver-tongued abolitionist had been delivering an unusually gloomy speech, asserting that only armed rebellion could free the slaves. "Slavery must end in blood!" he shouted. Truth, who believed that abolition could come peacefully, broke into Douglass's address with a simple but stunning question. "Frederick," she asked softly, "is God dead?" For many of those present, the idea suggested by Truth's question—that God lived, that hope was alive, that slavery could end without violence—threw a new light on the subject.

If Truth occasionally disagreed with Frederick Douglass, her words reflected no lack of esteem. She was one of the many thousands of Americans to whom this man represented larger-than-life heroism. Born into slavery in Maryland about 1817, Douglass learned

Highly intelligent but functionally illiterate, Sojourner Truth dictated her 1853 Narrative, *or autobiography, to a friend.*

basic reading from his owner's wife. When the owner heard about the lessons, he flew into a rage—knowledge of reading, he said, made a black unfit for his work—and forbade any further teaching. But with the head start he had been given, the young man went on to educate himself, first puzzling out signs and posters, then laboriously deciphering forbidden newspapers; by the time he was 16 he could read complex books (also, of course, forbidden). Douglass's independent attitude infuriated his master, who sent him to a "slave breaker," a man hired to destroy the spirit of a slave through beatings and intimidation. The effort failed: Douglass beat the slave breaker so severely that he never laid a hand on him again. Douglass later saw the episode as a watershed in his life. "I was nothing before; I was a man now," he said.

In 1838 Douglass proved his point. Rented by his master to a shipyard owner, he secretly obtained a

Citizens of Charleston, South Carolina, stage a raid on the U.S. Post Office about 1835. The angry southerners seized and burned thousands of abolitionist tracts mailed into the region by northern abolitionists.

certificate identifying its bearer as a free black seaman. He used this document to smuggle himself to New York, but he soon learned that for a black, that city could be as dangerous as any place in the South. Although New York State had outlawed slavery in 1827, the area swarmed with bounty hunters—men who seized escaped slaves and collected a reward for returning them to bondage.

Given shelter by David Ruggles of the New York Vigilance Committee, Douglass sent for his fiancée, Anna Murray. The free Maryland woman soon arrived and married Douglass, then accompanied him to a safer city: New Bedford, Massachusetts. There, one day in 1841, Douglass heard a lecture by the *Liberator*'s fiery publisher, William Lloyd Garrison, and it changed his life: he decided that he, too, would crusade for the abolition of slavery. A few days later he was called upon to speak himself. Facing a large abolitionist rally, he launched into a stirring recollection of his life as a slave—and electrified the audience. Garrison had been present, and when Douglass's powerful speech ended, he leapt to his feet. "Have we been listening to a thing," he asked, "or a man?" The audience shouted, "A man! A man!" Raising his voice, Garrison called out, "Shall such a man be held a slave in a Christian land?" "No! No!" roared the audience. "Shall such a man ever be sent back to bondage from the free soil of old Massachusetts?" shouted Garrison. The entire crowd sprang up and roared, "No! No! No!"

Douglass soon joined the American Anti-Slavery Society and began to lecture tirelessly. "As a speaker, he has few equals," asserted the Concord, Massachusetts, *Herald of Freedom*. "He has wit, arguments, sarcasm, pathos—all that first rate men show in their master efforts." Enhancing Douglass's dramatic performances were his personal characteristics: handsome and more than six feet tall, he had broad shoulders, a mass of flowing hair, flashing eyes, and a voice that rang like a trumpet. With his tales of brutal whippings and cruel treatment of black children and old people, Douglass moved audiences to tears. He could also make them laugh, especially when he described breaking the slave breaker, or when he imitated hypocritical ministers who told blacks to love God *and* servitude.

Seven years after he fled slavery, the former bondsman wrote a book, *Narrative of the Life of Frederick Douglass, an American Slave*. Still considered a remarkable document, the autobiography was a runaway best-seller in 1845. Nor was Douglass alone in attracting readers with a first-person account of slavery. Other freed blacks who wrote their life stories included William Wells Brown (1842), Lunsford Lane (1842), Moses Grandy (1844), Lewis Clark (1846), Henry Bibb (1849), and J. W. C. Pennington (1850).

Many of these autobiographers produced other successful works as well. In 1841, J. W. C. Pennington wrote *Textbook of the Origin and History of the Colored People*. In 1852, William Wells Brown described his travels in *Three Years in Europe*; he also wrote a play, *The Escape*, in 1858; a study of the Negro race, *The Black Man*, in 1863; and a history entitled *The Negro in the American Rebellions* in 1867. A regular contributor to the *Liberator* and the London *Daily News*, Brown was probably most celebrated for his best-selling novel, *Clotel; or, the President's Daughter*, published in 1853. This work, the first novel published by an African American, deals with the life of a black woman born to a white American president and his slave mistress. The plot is based on the legend that President Thomas Jefferson sired many children by the slaves on his Virginia plantation.

Meanwhile, Douglass's autobiography, which clearly identified its fugitive author, placed him in peril of recapture by his former master. When he got the chance to give a series of lectures in England, then, he jumped at the chance. His British speeches proved as mesmerizing as those he had delivered at home, enlisting thousands of Britons in the antislavery movement and other causes close to Douglass's heart. Along with abolition, he strongly supported rights for women and the temperance movement, which aimed at curbing the widespread abuse of alcoholic drinks.

Douglass rejoiced in his warm reception abroad. In England, he said in a letter to Garrison, "I breathe and lo! The chattel [property] becomes a man. I gaze around in vain for one who will question my human-

Frederick Douglass, 28 years old in this engraving, considered himself "nothing" until he was about 20. Only after he took charge of his own life—by beating a "slave breaker" almost to death—could he say, "I was a man now."

ity, claim me as a slave, or offer me an insult." Because Douglass remained a fugitive, a return to the United States would place him in danger of reenslavement, but he still felt obliged to go back and help those still in bondage. Then two English admirers solved his problem by raising the money to buy his freedom. In 1846 the 28-year-old·Douglass sailed for home, a free man.

Back in the United States, Douglass continued to lecture, often sharing the podium with Garrison. Although Garrison's paper, the *Liberator*, had a wide following, Douglass yearned to open his own, black-managed abolitionist publication, and in 1847 he did. Moving with his wife and children to Rochester, New York, he began publishing the *North Star*, a four-page weekly journal about slavery and abolition. Douglass ran the paper's motto across the masthead: "Right is of no sex—Truth is of no color—God is the Father of us all, and we are all Brethren." Assisting him in editing the *North Star* were his daughter, his three sons, and his friend Martin Delaney, a Harvard-educated physician, historian, novelist, and future black nationalist leader. Delaney's published works would include *The Condition, Elevation, Emigration and Destiny of the Colored People of the United States* (1852) and the novel *Blake; or, the Huts of America* (1859).

The *North Star* received high praise from both Americans and Britons, but praise could not pay for newsprint or salaries or children's food. To keep the paper—and his family—alive, Douglass used up his savings, mortgaged his house, and once again embarked on the lecture circuit. The black community helped, too. In Philadelphia, African American women held a fair to benefit the *North Star*. Selling used clothing, furniture, and baked goods, they raised $100—not enough to solve Douglass's financial problems, but an important symbol of black solidarity, a demonstration that blacks could pitch in together and support their own cause. African American contributions of this kind would help keep the journal going. Known as *Frederick Douglass' Paper* after 1851, it would continue publication until 1860, then survive for another three years as a monthly.

Douglass's newspaper was a milestone in black history; it marked the beginning of Douglass's independence from Garrison and other white abolitionists. Their help, of course, was essential to the cause, but many blacks wanted to demonstrate their ability to achieve their goals without white management. The *North Star* also helped Douglass meet other black leaders, in turn expanding those leaders' outlook. Douglass often disagreed strongly with colleagues such as Henry Highland Garnet, a supporter of black emigration to Liberia, but their arguments offered heartening proof of black strength. African American leaders were beginning to place themselves in the center of the events that would shape their people's lives.

By the close of the 1840s, Douglass had become one of the best known and most highly respected blacks in America. He was also one of the country's most in-demand lecturers, and had many times over proven himself a brilliant, highly independent thinker and a valiant defender of black rights. Douglass's reclaiming of his own manhood was, in a sense, a portent of freedom for millions of other black men and women.

7

THE FUGITIVE SLAVE LAW

Y the late 1840s the simmering rage between northern abolitionist and proslavery factions had approached the boiling point. In 1850 a new law—ironically, one designed to reduce the tensions—added more fuel to the fire.

The roots of this new law went back to 1848, when the United States had won a brief and costly war with Mexico. America's victory prizes included all of California and undisputed title to Texas (which had become the Union's 28th state in 1845, but which Mexico had never given up). Also part of the package—sweetened by a $15 million payment to Mexico—were the Utah and New Mexico territories, land that was to form all or part of six states: Nevada, Utah, New Mexico, Arizona, Wyoming, and Colorado.

California petitioned Congress for entry to the Union as a free (nonslave) state in 1849. Up to this point, states had always entered in pairs, one free, one slave, thus keeping the balance between the North and South as even as possible. The idea of California's

Worldly goods over his shoulder, a determined runaway makes his way north. In the four decades before passage of the 1850 Fugitive Slave Law, some 2,000 slaves had evaporated into the North or Canada each year. They kept on trying, but after the law, escape became increasingly difficult and dangerous.

Neither am I a friend to Duelling, not I!

Never mind, I hold a cool Sixty Slaves myself & "I will continue to oppose any scheme, whatever of emancipation, gradual or immediate".

Yet I take a shot whenever it suits me.

admission as a free state produced howls of outrage from the South. Such a move, said southerners, would shift the political balance to the northern side, and the South could not and would not stand for it. For decades, farseeing Americans had been haunted by the notion that the philosophical and economic differences between North and South would divide the

Well done Hal, your old folly & delusi
Liberty are gone. You are beginning
in its true light "as the most safe
for free institutions in the world".
shake of your daddle my worthy
made President for life.

s Line.

In this contemporary political cartoon, proslavery senator John C. Calhoun (right) congratulates Senator Henry Clay, author of the 1850 Fugitive Slave Law, for "beginning to see slavery in its true light." The politicians seem unconcerned about the suffering black man under their feet.

young nation. At this point, the specter of a deadly civil war seemed to glide just a little closer.

Stepping in to save the day—at least for the time being—was Henry Clay, a silver-tongued Kentucky senator aptly nicknamed the Great Pacificator (peacemaker). Clay's solution to the complex and explosive problem was, typically, a compromise. First, he said,

admit California as a free state (one point for the North). Next, let the New Mexico and Utah territories remain open to slavery and, when they applied for statehood, decide if they wished to be free or slave. (Basically, this was another point for the North; everyone knew the territories would outlaw slavery as soon as they could.) To keep the South from bolting the Union on the spot, Clay offered two concessions. First, although slave trading would become illegal in Washington, D.C., the practice of slavery there could continue. Second—and most important—Congress would revise an old law, the Fugitive Slave Law of 1793, giving it drastic new sweep and strength. (Al-

Captioned "A northern freeman enslaved by northern hands," this Anti-Slavery Almanac *illustration shows four white men subduing a helpless black man. Bounty hunting had been going on for years, but after the Fugitive Slave Law, the sinister trade became big business.*

ways hard to enforce, the 1793 act lost most of its bite when the U.S. Supreme Court ruled in 1842 that the law did not oblige state officials to help in recovering runaway slaves.)

Strangely enough, most of those who proposed and backed the Fugitive Slave Law had no love for slavery; on the contrary, many wanted to end it. But their first goal was to keep the United States from flying apart. For these people, the Fugitive Slave Law was a temporary and necessary compromise, and they pushed it through the legislative body. Congress approved Clay's proposal, known as the Compromise of 1850, on September 18.

Under the new Fugitive Slave Law, any African American, anywhere in the United States, could be accused of escaping slavery and forcibly brought before a special commissioner. If the accuser swore to be the black person's legal owner or the owner's representative, the commissioner could return the black to slavery. If the slave resisted, or if abolitionists tried to rescue him or her, the self-styled owner could demand a guard of federal officers to accompany his party south. The alleged fugitive was allowed neither a jury trial nor the right to testify on her or his own behalf. The new law also decreed that anyone, white or black, who was convicted of aiding a fugitive slave could be fined $1,000, ordered to pay an additional $1,000 in "civil damages" to the slave's owner, and jailed for six months.

Abolitionists called the law unjust and intolerable. "It seemed now," wrote Harriet Beecher Stowe, future author of the antislavery novel *Uncle Tom's Cabin*, "as if the system once confined to the Southern States was rousing itself . . . to extend itself all over the North, and to overgrow the institutions of free society." Others bitterly denounced the government for, as one newspaper put it, "acquiring the morals and behavior of a slave trader."

Even nonabolitionists rose up against the law, pointing out that it violated the Constitution's Sixth Amendment, which guarantees any accused person the right to trial by jury, the right to summon favorable witnesses, and the right to a lawyer. Furthermore, said the act's opponents, it encouraged corruption among the special commissioners, who were to be paid twice as much for issuing a warrant for a slave's arrest as they were for releasing a free black person who had been

CAUTION!!

COLORED PEOPLE

OF BOSTON, ONE & ALL,

You are hereby respectfully CAUTIONED and advised, to avoid conversing with the

Watchmen and Police Officers of Boston,

For since the recent ORDER OF THE MAYOR & ALDERMEN, they are empowered to act as

KIDNAPPERS

AND

Slave Catchers,

And they have already been actually employed in KIDNAPPING, CATCHING, AND KEEPING SLAVES. Therefore, if you value your LIBERTY, and the *Welfare of the Fugitives* among you, *Shun* them in every possible manner, as so many *HOUNDS* on the track of the most unfortunate of your race.

Keep a Sharp Look Out for KIDNAPPERS, and have TOP EYE open.

APRIL 24, 1851.

THEODORE PARKER'S PLACARD

Placard written by Theodore Parker and printed and posted by the Vigilance Committee of Boston after the rendition of Thomas Sims to slavery in April, 1851.

Advising Boston's "Colored People" to practice "CAUTION!!", posters like this one appeared all over Boston after the April 1851 capture of Thomas Sims. The escaped slave had spent several peaceful years working in Boston before the new Fugitive Slave Law legalized his forced return to the South.

falsely arrested. The new law also allowed U.S. marshals to hire posses—groups of ordinary citizens—to arrest runaways. These federally empowered posses could override local authority, giving slave owners the rights they had sought for years. Because slave hunting was now easier and cheaper, the owners could afford to go after all their missing slaves, including less "valuable" ones such as the scarred, rebellious Harriet Tubman.

Planters now offered rewards for the return of their runaways, creating a new breed of professional slave-catcher in the North. Bounty hunters opened store-front offices and offered to pursue escaped slaves for a $10 down payment and a $100 success fee. Posters went up everywhere as the greatest manhunt in American history got under way. Because even a free African American could be handed over to any-one claiming his or her ownership, no black was safe. More than one free American was dragged off into a life of slavery simply for having black skin.

To resist the hated law, abolitionists went into high gear. In Boston, New York, and other northern cities, they formed watchdog groups to warn blacks when bounty hunters were spotted. Under the aboli-tionists' influence several northern states, starting with Vermont in 1850, passed a series of "personal liberty laws," which in effect nullified the Fugitive Slave Law. Under these liberty laws, alleged fugitives received lawyers, jury trials, and the right to introduce evidence to defend themselves.

Free blacks in the North also rallied to the cause of the fugitives. Leading this black move-ment was Frederick Douglass, who noted that most whites regarded blacks as meek and unwill-ing to fight. "This reproach must be wiped out," he said, "and nothing short of resistance on the part of the colored man can wipe it out. Every slavehunter who meets a bloody death in his infernal business is an argument in favor of the manhood of our race."

Northern hostility was increased by the sight of southern slaveholders searching for blacks who had lived peacefully in the North for years. In some Yan-kee cities, abolitionists tried—often with success—to seize captured runaways and arrange their escape. The North's attitude angered and frightened the South, whose politicians rent the air with cries of protest. Considering the fact that the actual number of slaves who managed successful escapes was relatively small, the South's outcry against northerners' aid to fugitives seemed all the more extreme to the North.

The South's uproar, in fact, served to push previously neutral northerners into the abolition camp. The "antislavery community," observes biographer William S. McFeely in his *Frederick Douglass* (1991), "grew larger as a result of [enforcement of the Fugitive Slave Law]. The spectacle of people being condemned by federal commissioners and marched by federal troops to ships that would carry them back to slavery in the South aroused northern opposition to slavery as nothing else had. Slavery had become visible—as Douglass, with his verbal descriptions, had long sought to make it."

Meanwhile, in spite of antislavery sentiment, and in spite of their high personal reputations, free blacks such as Frederick Douglass were facing widespread racial discrimination. From the time of his first arrival in New York, Douglass had taken a hands-on approach to Jim Crow laws. When traveling by train, for example, the abolitionist leader routinely seated himself in the first-class car, which was off-limits to blacks even in the "liberal" North. Invariably, the train conductor would ask him to go back to the third-class coach, and just as invariably Douglass would refuse to move. What followed often involved the conductor and his aides roughly dragging Douglass out of the car.

Many of Douglass's white friends expressed bewilderment about his behavior in these circumstances. How, they asked, could this man, who spoke so reasonably about the evils of slavery, act in such a confrontational manner? Rather than understanding Douglass's acts as a form of passive resistance, many people saw them as unnecessary agitation. Did he not realize, they asked, that whites would not change their laws because of the resistance of one unarmed man? Why did he do it? Douglass had this answer in 1849:

> **"Those who profess to favor freedom and yet deprecate agitation are men who want crops without plowing up the ground. They want rain without thunder and lightning. They want the ocean without the awful roar of its many waters. The struggle may be a moral one; or it may be a physical one; or it may be both moral and physical, but it must be a struggle. Power concedes nothing without a demand. It never did and it never will."**

For Douglass and many other blacks, it was important to demonstrate moral courage in the face of unjust laws. By requiring whites to carry their racism to its logical conclusion—in this case dragging Douglass bodily from a train seat—he required them to think about their actions. Whites who witnessed such a scene had to ponder it as well. Douglass believed that, over time, racism would be defeated by its own ugliness. In the not very distant future, an American president would agree. Talking of slavery in 1860, Abraham Lincoln was to predict that "the hateful institution, like a reptile poisoning itself, will perish by its own infamy."

Not until 13 years after passage of the Fugitive Slave Law—and 32 years after Nat Turner's revolt—would Lincoln's Emancipation Proclamation free the South's slaves. But the events that began in 1831 and ended with that fugitive law would lead, as sure as the sun rose, to America's Civil War (1860–65) and the final liberation of all Americans.

When Nat Turner raised his ax on that hot summer night, he had no idea, of course, that he was

The years that followed Nat Turner's revolt unveiled a galaxy of heroic Americans: visionaries and activists, adventurers and writers, lofty idealists and practical politicians. One man was all of these. No single individual— black or white—emerges from this period with the towering grandeur of Frederick Douglass.

setting in motion a chain of events that would shape history. The same probably holds true for Frederick Douglass, Harriet Tubman, Sojourner Truth, and the legion of other heroes who rose to strike their blows for liberty. We know who some of them are, and we have heard of some of their countless deeds of courage; many more bold men and women and many more daring acts, performed by a people determined to break their chains, will remain forever unknown. Nevertheless, we know of the dreams they dreamed and the price they paid. We see what they wrought, how far we have come—and how far we must still go. And whenever America marches forward, through days of sorrow and years of glory, they will march too.

FURTHER READING

Bennett, Lerone, Jr. *Before the Mayflower: A History of Black America 1619–1964*. Baltimore: Penguin Books, 1984.

Bisson, Terry. *Nat Turner*. New York: Chelsea House, 1988.

Borzendowski, Janice. *John Russworm*. New York: Chelsea House, 1989.

Celsi, Teresa. *John C. Calhoun and the Roots of Civil War*. New York: Silver Burdett Press, 1991.

Collins, James L. *John Brown and the Fight Against Slavery*. Brookfield, CT: Millbrook Press, 1991.

Franklin, John Hope, with Alfred Moss. *From Slavery to Freedom: A History of Negro Americans*. New York: Knopf, 1987.

McClard, Megan. *Harriet Tubman: Slavery and the Underground Railroad*. New York: Silver Burdett Press, 1991.

McFeely, William S. *Frederick Douglass*. New York: Norton, 1991.

Shumate, Jane. *Sojourner Truth and the Voice of Freedom*. Brookfield, CT: Millbrook Press, 1991.

Simms, Henry H. *Emotion at High Tide: Abolition as a Controversial Factor, 1830–1845*. New York: University Place, 1960.

Taylor, M. W. *Harriet Tubman*. New York: Chelsea House, 1991.

INDEX

PICTURE CREDITS

TIMOTHY J. PAULSON, who lives and works in New York City, has written several children's books, including *How To Fly a 747* and *The Beanstalk Incident*. Cofounder of Agincourt Press, where he produced more than 70 volumes for young adults, Paulson is currently working on a book about vintage motorcycles.

CLAYBORNE CARSON, senior consulting editor of the MILESTONES IN BLACK AMERICAN HISTORY series, is a professor of history at Stanford University. His first book, *In Struggle: SNCC and the Black Awakening of the 1960s* (1981), won the Frederick Jackson Turner Prize of the Organization of American Historians. He is the director of the Martin Luther King, Jr., Papers Project, which will publish 12 volumes of King's writings.

DARLENE CLARK HINE, senior consulting editor of the MILESTONES IN BLACK AMERICAN HISTORY series, is the John A. Hannah Professor of American History at Michigan State University. She is the author of numerous books and articles on black women's history. Her most recent work is the two-volume *Black Women in America: An Historical Encyclopedia* (1993).